PELICAN BOOKS

DEFOE TO THE VICTORIANS

Two Centuries of the English Novel

David Skilton was born in London in 1942 and
educated at King's College, Cambridge, and at the
University of Copenhagen. He has been a lecturer at
the Universities of Stockholm and Glasgow, and is
now Professor of English at SDUC, Lampeter, in
the University of Wales. He is the author of *Anthony
Trollope and his Contemporaries: A Study in the
Theory and Conventions of Mid-Victorian Realism*
(1972), and has edited Thomas Hardy's *Tess of the
d'Urbervilles* for the Penguin English Library and
co-edited (with Peter Miles) Anthony Trollope's
Framley Parsonage (Penguin English Library) and
Wilkie Collins's *The Woman in White*. He has also
written introductions and notes for several books
and a variety of articles, in particular on Victorian
literature.

DAVID SKILTON

*

DEFOE
TO THE
VICTORIANS

Two Centuries of the English Novel

Penguin Books

To the memory of my mother

Penguin Books Ltd, Harmondsworth, Middlesex, England
Viking Penguin Inc., 40 West 23rd Street, New York, New York 10010, U.S.A.
Penguin Books Australia Ltd, Ringwood, Victoria, Australia
Penguin Books Canada Ltd, 2801 John Street, Markham, Ontario, Canada L3R 1B4
Penguin Books (N.Z.) Ltd, 182–190 Wairau Road, Auckland 10, New Zealand

First published in Great Britain by David & Charles, and
simultaneously in the U.S.A. by Barnes & Noble
(a division of Harper & Row Publishers Inc.), 1977
Published in Pelican Books 1985

Printed and bound in Great Britain by
Cox & Wyman Ltd, Reading
Set in Monotype Garamond

Contents

I am grateful to the Librarian and staff of Glasgow University Library for their friendly assistance, and to numerous friends and colleagues, including Liz Atkinson, Marcella Evaristi, David McKie, Gordon Phillips, Michal Scollen, Mary Sillitto and Ingrid Swanson.

CHAPTER 1

Defoe and the Augustan Age

Reading the novels of Daniel Defoe in the context of other major works from the early eighteenth century reveals a great contrast between the unselfconscious realism of Defoe's fiction and the highly self-conscious neo-classical mode of satire which predominated among contemporary poets, and between a celebration of the revolutionary capitalist virtues of work and profit on the one hand, and the aristocratic myth of hierarchy and obedience on the other. The emergence of realistic prose fiction as a major literary form in English is inextricably involved in the social and cultural conflict this contrast reveals.

At the end of *The Dunciad*, Pope presents a vision of the triumph of Dulness, the goddess of Dunces, hacks and Grub Street scribblers:

> Lo! the great Anarch's ancient reign restor'd,
> Light dies before her uncreating word:
> . . .
>
> Thus at her felt approach, and secret might,
> Art after Art goes out, and all is Night.
> . . .
>
> Thy hand great Dulness! lets the curtain fall,
> And universal Darkness covers all.
>
> (*Dunciad Variorum*, III, 339–40, 345–6 and 355–6)

This is, of course, a comic vision of Dulness blotting out litera-

7

ture, art and science from the world: a mock-heroic triumph of the goddess as the culmination of a long ironic celebration of the forces of modernity, which Pope so much despised. Yet, despite the comedy, there was in the modern world something that Pope not only disliked but seriously feared, and *The Dunciad*, for all the poet's assumption of superiority, shows a real fear of an approaching cataclysm, when there really might rise

> . . . the Seed of Chaos, and of Night,
> To blot out Order, and extinguish Light,
> Of dull and venal a new World to mold,
> And bring Saturnian days of Lead and Gold.
>   (1742 version, IV, 13–16)

Although nothing in *The Dunciad* can be taken at face value, the final impression is that the world of Augustan humanism is seriously threatened by forces of cultural change. 'Do not gentle reader,' Martinus Scriblerus exhorts us, in a note to the first lines above, 'rest too secure in thy contempt of the Instruments for such a revolution in learning, or despise such weak agents as have been described in our poem, but remember what the *Dutch* stories somewhere relate, that a great part of their Provinces was once overflow'd, by a small opening made in one of their dykes by a single *Water-Rat*.' Though apparently secure, the Augustan cultural world is very precarious, threatened by the meanest rodent of a Grub Street hack, and the image of order shored up against chaos is a neo-classical commonplace.

It was in the world described by Swift and Pope that the novels of Daniel Defoe first appeared—books which we now regard as the first English novels in the modern sense of the word—and, in order to appreciate the challenge they offered to the Augustan establishment, it will be necessary to look at the leading assumptions of Augustan humanism, as held variously by Swift, Pope and, later, Samuel Johnson. The major premise of early eighteenth-century humanism is that there exists an immutable human essence, usually known as 'human nature', that this 'human nature' is historically invariable, and our understanding of it embodied in western literature from Homer onwards.

'Human nature' is held to possess great potential for dignity, nobility and comprehension of the divine order, standing as it does only a little below the angels in the ordained scheme of things; but it is also essentially corrupt since the Fall. As Samuel Johnson says, 'Man's chief merit consists in resisting the impulses of his nature', for, according to the Augustan thinker, only in the recognition of its own limitations can the full value of human nature be seen. This view required the resigned acceptance of in-built contradiction in existence—the recognition, in the terms of Book IV of Swift's *Gulliver's Travels*, of both the Houyhnhnm and the Yahoo in man—so that Augustan humanism frequently implies a violent human self-disgust, and leads to extreme polarisations of good and evil, dignity and filth, expressed in such pleasant dicta as 'Woman is a Temple built over a sewer'.

In addition, the Augustan humanist believes he has sufficient historical evidence of the invariability of human nature to reject the notion of progress in the world. His optimism tells him that 'Whatever is, is RIGHT' and that, although there may be advances in mathematics or canal-building, mankind cannot be improved in the moral sphere, which for him is the core of human existence. On the other hand there were a number of important writers— Defoe prominent among them—who pursued a progressive line of thought, believing that the condition of mankind could be essentially improved. As the century continued, progressive views were to dominate European thought, leading on eventually in extreme forms to such things as the perfectibilism behind the French Revolution, or the millennial vision of Blake's prophetic books. A progressive attitude, unambiguous in Defoe, can be seen uneasily coexisting with the older Augustan mode of thought in a writer like Richardson, who, though a High Church Tory, believed in greater personal freedom within a set scheme of things, and who was more conscious of the linguistic heritage of Shake-speare and the Authorised Version than of the cultural tradition

of the classical languages. For Pope and his like, classical literature contained the highest cultural authority, but like many other
progressive thinkers Defoe was not classically educated, having
received a thoroughly modern schooling at a dissenting academy.
Taken all round, Defoe represented at once a social, literary and
intellectual challenge to the Augustan world, and the Augustans
reacted to him accordingly.

Pope and Swift objected to Defoe in no uncertain terms. For
Swift he was 'the Fellow that was *pilloryed*, I have forgot his
Name', while Pope enrols him among the dunces of *The Dunciad*.
The fact that Defoe was put in the pillory in 1703 for a hugely
ironic anti-High Church polemic, *The Shortest-Way with the
Dissenters*, indicates clearly enough that he and his like repre-
sented a real threat to the established order of things.

The Augustan vision of the world was a philosophical and
religious construct based on a myth of the eternal fitness of things,
as celebrated by Dryden and Nathaniel Lee:

> Whatever is, is in its causes just;
> . . . But purblind man
> Sees but a part o' the chain; the nearest link;
> His eyes not carrying to that equal beam,
> That poses all above.
> (*Oedipus*, 1679, III, i)

Man had his place in the Great Chain of Being above the animals
and a little lower than the angels, and in the human world too
everyone had his proper place on a divinely appointed social scale.
Although Pope's *Dunciad* was largely an attack on bad literature,
it was also a response to economic developments in the world of
letters which threatened the received order in the same way as
commercialism and capitalism threatened the idea of ordered
social stability which Augustanism celebrated. The rout of the
dunces takes place on Lord Mayor's Day and follows the route of
his procession. The equation of bad art and social disruption with
the commercial classes could hardly be clearer and, for Pope,

Grub Street not only stands for cultural decay but for social and moral collapse as well. Pope and Swift basically objected to Defoe as a representative of the City, who embodied the social as much as the aesthetic aspects of the Grubean threat.

As a dissenter, as tradesman and merchant, a bankrupt ship-insurer, a political agent, a pamphleteer and one of our first modern journalists, Daniel Defoe ran counter to the Augustan myth of order in most of his life and work, and his career displays clearly the distinctively modern aspects of the early eighteenth century. *The Dunciad* embodied a great deal of social and literary fact when it saw the ideals of culture and civilisation as Pope understood them threatened by a rising tide of commercialism and individualism. Believing that they themselves possessed the truth, the Augustans could not entertain any other system of thought, but in this battle of the books it was the moderns who would ultimately have their triumph.

Whatever else its object, *The Life and Strange Surprizing Adventures of Robinson Crusoe, of York, Mariner*, which came out in 1719, was not calculated to make a favourable impression on the world of polite letters. It ran through four editions in a few months, as well as a pirated edition, selling principally among Defoe's fellow-citizens and fellow-dissenters, among them some of the poorest among the literate, to judge from contemporary comments. Charles Gildon for one sneered that Crusoe was 'fam'd from *Tuttle-Street* to *Limehouse-hole*; there is not an old Woman that can go to the Price of it, but buys [his] *Life and Adventures*, and leaves it as a Legacy, with the *Pilgrims Progress* . . . to her Posterity'.

Defoe was nearly sixty, with about 400 previous publications, large and small, behind him when he published *Robinson Crusoe*, continuing it five months later with *The Farther Adventures*; it was closely followed in the next four years by the new fictional ventures of *Captain Singleton, Moll Flanders, Colonel Jack* and *Roxana*. What we now regard as the earliest English novels were written within a few years, towards the end of a life crowded with other literary, commercial and political activities.

Even had they been inclined to, Pope, Swift and their associates could not have taken Defoe's new form of prose fiction seriously, since their classically-based critical categories could not embrace it. In classical terms the novel is a bastard form, and much of the theorising about it in the next century and a half is aimed at making the form respectable. Ideologically too there is a striking contrast between Defoe's progressive and Pope's conservative visions of the world. Augustanism was an aristocratic myth, fiercely protective of the status quo, and necessitating the defence of an intellectual order that was already departing, while Defoe and others of his class and persuasion stood for revolutionary change, for economic individualism, social mobility, trade and industry, and freedom of conscience. Defoe developed his sort of novel as a literary form which could embody these things—the ideals of his class.

Defoe's novels are all first-person accounts of the lives of social deviants—criminals or adventurers. In their old age, reformed and supposedly repentant, his protagonists tell their stories with unconcealed gusto, interspersing their accounts with bouts of moralising. They relate their lives mainly in terms of changes in their social status, financial condition and the states of their souls or consciences. Character and behaviour are to a great degree controlled by environment, not by the laws of an immutable 'human nature', and Defoe's explanations of human phenomena are more circumstantial than psychological.

In *Robinson Crusoe* Defoe created not only a work of fiction but one of the major myths of western civilisation. The island scenes, describing the survival of an isolated man, thrown back entirely on his own resources—aided by a fair complement of tools and materials saved from two wrecks, of course—has always had the greatest imaginative impact, and the spirit of mercantile capitalism is enshrined in this unprepossessing but strangely sympathetic adventurer.

All Defoe's novels are in part a celebration of industry and trade, and moderate prosperity and comfort in the 'middle station' of life, which Robinson Crusoe's father considers 'the best State in the World, the most suited to human Happiness, not exposed to the Miseries and Hardships, the Labour and Sufferings of the mechanick Part of Mankind, and not embarass'd with the Pride, Luxury, Ambition and Envy of the upper Part of Mankind' (*Robinson Crusoe*, OEN, p4). Because of his 'wandring Inclination', Crusoe needlessly disobeys both God and his father in setting out on his foreign travels and, ignoring the warnings which Providence sends him in the shape of a succession of lesser disasters, he persists until he is thrown up alone on his island for twenty-eight years' penance. His offence is both social and religious in not heeding the example of Agur, who 'prayed to have neither Poverty or Riches' (OEN, p4; Proverbs, xxx.8), but although the religious pattern of his 'reluctant pilgrimage' is clear, the ostensibly spiritual aspect of the book has proved to be difficult to interpret. In all Defoe's novels the problem is whether the religious and secular thoughts of the protagonist are compatible. Does the character's unmistakable love of material gain invalidate his interspersed moments of religious thought? If so, is the religion and morality merely a sop to Defoe's puritan readership? After all, when Defoe's adventurers finally repent their lives of crime, he often allows them to keep their ill-gotten wealth. Social salvation seems as important as religious salvation. On the other hand, is it the religious experience that is central to the fiction, and could the pursuit of money and material comfort really be secondary? In other words, the uncertainty about a Defoe novel is whether, in the language of the preface to *Colonel Jack*, it constitutes a fictional 'history' or a 'parable'.

The religious pattern of *Robinson Crusoe* is clear enough, and many more of Crusoe's religious reflections fall in pat with the surrounding action than do those of Moll Flanders, Colonel Jack or Roxana. It is part of the normal exercise of the puritan mind to enquire into the providential significance of worldly things and happenings, and in his progress from disobedience to repentance Crusoe places a more and more religious interpretation on events. Admittedly his moral tone is often too complacent or fulsome for modern taste, and sometimes the dissenting preacher can be clearly heard—as, for example, when Crusoe remembers that he alone was saved in the shipwreck:

> Well, you are in a desolate Condition 'tis true, but pray remember, Where are the rest of you? Did not you come Eleven of you into the Boat, where are the Ten? Why were not they sav'd and you lost? Why were you singled out? Is it better to be here or there? and then I pointed to the Sea. All Evills are to be consider'd with the Good that is in them, and with what worse attends them.

(OEN, pp62–3)

Sermons were a major and respectable influence on English prose in the eighteenth century—the nonconformist sermon on Defoe (sometimes, as here, complete with gestures), and the Latitudinarian Church of England sermon on Fielding and the essayists. Defoe's preaching is part of his cultural inheritance.

In the other novels, the allegorical framework is hidden under a welter of factual detail concerning the protagonists' lives of crime and acquisition. Because of Moll Flanders' loving catalogues of her gains, her account of her own repentance does not convincingly add up to an improving moral tale: her moralising sits too lightly on her throughout her story. It is not easy for us to regard these novels as coherent moral tales, but in spite of the conflict between moral and spiritual attitudes—indeed, because of it—the protagonists make perfectly good sense as credible fictional persons. In *Robinson Crusoe* Defoe created a fable of great power, but he did it by removing his hero far out of the social system and, for large tracts of the book, from any contact at all with his fellow men. In such a highly artificial fictional world it was possible to laboratory-test the puritan ethic, but in a complex fictional world involving a full set of social and economic relationships a protagonist's puritan morality could not operate for long without revealing its inherent contradictions. It is not that Defoe failed as an individual writer in not reconciling the spiritual and the mundane aspects of the puritan outlook, but that out of the conflict of the two there had emerged a secularised puritan consciousness. Defoe was expressing with particular clarity something that was common to his class and sect.

An incompatibility between the tenor of a narrative and the moral inference the teller claims to draw from it was not, of course, a new thing with Defoe, nor limited to dissenting protestant literature. His greatest predecessors in realistic first-person prose narrative, the picaresque novelists of the Spanish golden age, had been caught in the same conflict between the narrator's stated moral and that implicit in the tale. The most important of these authors—for our purposes, at least—was Mateo Alemán, whose influential *Life of Guzmán de Alfarache* belonged to the literary wing of the Counter-Reformation. After a chastening spell in the galleys, the criminal Guzmán, now penitent, gleefully recounts his former misdeeds for the improvement rather than the diversion of his readers, or so he would have us believe. Alemán is aware of the strain his fiction is under from the moral antinomy inherent in his narrative method and, in the 1623 English translation by James Mabbe, Guzmán says,

> Some perhaps will say, That having (like unto Watermen) turned my backe and eyes the contrarie way, (who looke one way, and rowe another) I direct this little Barke of mine, where I have most desire to land. But upon mine honest word . . . it was my sole purpose, to guide the prow for the publicke good . . .

The importance of early Spanish picaresque novels to Defoe and subsequent English fiction will be discussed later. For the moment it is enough to notice how two writers with vastly different aims and beliefs find the same difficulty in reconciling realism with morality.

In Defoe's case this conflict within the fiction is particularly interesting because he offers simultaneous social and religious interpretations of his people's lives. For Crusoe there is little contradiction. Disobedience to his father is at the same time disobedience to the will of God. His error is in not contentedly remaining in the 'middle station of life' into which he was born, and thus avoiding the snares of both poverty and riches. In eighteenth-century sermons the verse from the Book of Proverbs which Crusoe's father quotes at him was commonly used to connect material sufficiency with spiritual well-being. But Moll Flanders and Colonel Jack, both children of whores and starting their lives at the bottom of the social scale, and Roxana, who sets out on her delinquent career when penniless and defenceless, all frequently quote a biblical tag with a very different emphasis: 'Give me not poverty lest I steal.'

This and the elder Crusoe's are in fact parts of the same text, Proverbs, xxx.8–9: '. . . give me neither poverty nor riches . . . Lest I be full, and deny thee, and say, Who is the LORD? or lest I be poor, and steal, and take the name of my God in vain'. This must be counted as Defoe's favourite text, and is a key to a whole socio-religious complex of English bourgeois thought. As used by Defoe's characters it succinctly explains the workings of social 'necessity'—that force which makes the unfortunate into the criminal, and also makes us sympathetic towards the criminal. Moll's case is typical. Like Colonel Jack she has ever since a child had an overwhelming desire for the security that only social advancement could give. She 'wanted to be plac'd in a settled State of Living . . . [and] the Vice came in always at the Door of Necessity, not at the Door of Inclination' (OEN, pp128–9).

There is in Defoe a genuine sympathy with the poor and the oppressed—of his own race, at any rate—such as is not met with again in prose fiction until Dickens. But, in Defoe's bourgeois vision, only individual solutions are possible to major social problems. Yet he sometimes very movingly puts the case of the miserably deprived: Colonel Jack's childhood is a notable example. Here he is being questioned by a gentleman:

What doest thou do for thy Living?

16

> I go Errands, *said I*, for the Folks in
> *Rosemary-lane*.
> And what dost thou do for a Lodging
> at Night?
> I lye at the Glass-House, *said I*,
> at Night.
> How lye at the Glass-House! have they
> any Beds there? *says he*.
> I never lay in a Bed in my Life, *said I*,
> as I remember.
> Why? *says he*, what do you lye on at
> the Glass-House?
> The Ground, *says I*, and sometimes a little
> Straw, or upon the warm Ashes.
>
> (OEN, pp36–7)

Outside Dickens, the point of view of a child, and particularly a miserably deprived child, is nowhere better put and this passage illustrates Defoe's gift of immediacy in direct speech too, which he matches with an equally fluid colloquial narrative. The social moral of *Colonel Jack* and *Moll Flanders* reaches no farther than a humane appeal for more and more enlightened charities to cut down human suffering, and elsewhere, when Roxana vigorously protests against the subjugation of women, her problem defies solution in Defoe's universe, and must be dropped as suddenly as it has arisen (OEN, pp146–53). Defoe's sympathies take him into areas where he knows no answers to the questions he encounters.

His narrative carries irresistible conviction through the recognisable colloquial manner of the narrator and the strict attention given to corroborative detail, for Defoe is a master of circumstantial authenticity. He uses similar techniques in much of his nonfiction too, and in terms of literary method it is misleading to draw a fast distinction between his factual and his fictional writings. Even in his purely historical works he often hides behind a slenderly characterised mouthpiece, such as the 'Scots Gentleman in the Swedish Service' who supposedly writes *The*

History of the Wars of Charles XII (1715). When the narrator is more fully realised as a fictional personality, Defoe produces brilliant documentary fiction like *Memoirs of a Cavalier* (1720), or *A Journal of the Plague Year* (1722), one of the most involving documentaries ever written. As well as approximating to Defoe's original middle-class readership in social terms, the saddler who recounts the events of the Great Plague of 1665 is so unassuming and so detailed that it is impossible not to credit his stories. One cannot disbelieve the friendly voice of a man who introduces himself as living 'without *Aldgate* about mid-way between *Aldgate Church* and *White-Chappel-Bars*, on the left Hand or North-side of the Street' (OEN, p7). In fact Defoe so mastered the art of convincing by circumstantial detail that his *True Relation of the Apparition of one Mrs. Veal, the next day after her death: to one Mrs. Bargrave, at Canterbury* (1705) was one of the most credited ghost stories of the century.

In *Moll Flanders, Colonel Jack* and *Roxana* Defoe presents London so authentically that his novels constitute social records as well as fictions. His approach to London can best be appreciated by contrasting it with Pope's treatment of the City in *The Dunciad*, in which actual geography is used for the purpose of moral symbolism. For example, Rosemary Lane was a flea-market and a haunt of prostitutes in one of the poorest parts of town, near the Tower. For Colonel Jack it is a place where he runs errands and is paid in food and old clothes. For Pope in the 1728 version of *The Dunciad* it is a symbol of social and moral degradation. These two approaches show the contrast between the bourgeois and the Augustan ways of regarding the City, and by extension the world. The possibility of a vision which would unite the realistic with the symbolic approach is not fully realised until Blake (in 'London', say) or Dickens.

CHAPTER 2

Richardson and Fielding

SAMUEL RICHARDSON

Two decades after Defoe's novels a very different development in the history of English fiction came with the publication of Samuel Richardson's *Pamela* in 1740; once again what distinguished the new work from the mass of previous prose fiction was its realistic treatment of the contemporary world while, like Defoe, Richardson too projected the ideology of his class and age. Defoe and Richardson were both tradesmen and citizens of London, but there the resemblance ends. Against Defoe, the progressive dissenter, we can set Richardson, the High Church Tory; and against Defoe, the pilloried pamphleteer, the government agent and the man of the world, Richardson is the sober, domestic, self-consciously upright master-printer, who boasted unembarrassedly of his morals and could claim that 'I never, to my Knowledge, was . . . in Company with a lewd Woman, in my Life'. Yet the important thing about both writers, historically speaking, is that they expressed ways in which the world was seen by an independent middle class. Both had a profound respect for the capitalist virtues, and Richardson considered England to be 'a Kingdom which owes its Support, and the Figure it makes abroad, intirely to Trade; the Followers of which are infinitely of more Consequence, and deserve more to be incourag'd, than any other Degree or Rank of People in it'. The emergence of the

English novel shows the growing influence of a middle-class vision in our literature. While rule-bound verse-forms backed by traditional authority would be the natural vehicle for older, hierarchic modes of thought, the bastard form of the novel could adapt itself to new interpretations of the world.

Pamela, or Virtue Rewarded is one of the most famous stories ever written of male stratagems thwarted by female prudence. It relates a squire's repeated attempts on the virtue of one of his late mother's servants, and is told entirely in letters, written largely by the girl, Pamela, herself. Pamela displays such perfection in resisting her master's advances that he ends by marrying her. A second part to the novel, published some time later in 1742, shows how, having been elevated from her previous humble station, she now proceeds to win over the neighbouring gentry and aristocracy by her domestic and moral excellence. We have Richardson's own account of how he came to write *Pamela*. Two booksellers, he said, 'had long been urging me to give them a little book . . . of familiar letters on the useful concerns in common life . . . And, among the rest, I thought of giving one or two as cautions to young folks circumstanced as Pamela was'. Deciding to expand enormously on such an idea, he hoped to turn prose fiction away from 'the pomp and parade of romance-writing', by replacing 'the improbable and marvellous' of the earlier romances of chivalry by lessons in 'religion and virtue'. His 'new species of writing' made the epistolary novel the important form it was in England and France throughout the eighteenth century.

The success of *Pamela* was immediate. The close identification which the epistolary novel induced with the heroine in her distress and the unparalleled attention Richardson paid to the minutiae of daily life ravished his readers, while the pervasive tone of moral rectitude provided a convenient and much-needed rationale for the otherwise dubious taste for prose fiction. For Aaron Hill, a habitually emphatic friend of the author, Richardson was 'a salutary *Angel*, in *Sodom*', but not all his contemporaries were so happy with the morality of his novel. For some it was disgustingly prurient in its concentration on a young virgin's sexual charms, while some scenes in it were distinctly 'warm'; and the French translation of part one of *Pamela* remained on the *Index* of prohibited books until 1900, when it was replaced by the English original.

There were readers too who disputed whether it were not artful deceit rather than 'virtue' that was rewarded in Pamela's advantageous marriage. In *Shamela* (1741), a witty burlesque on *Pamela* which purported to uncover the servant-girl's hypocrisy, Henry Fielding used the phonetically vulgar spelling 'vartue' throughout, in order to suggest something radically false in the morality of Richardson's book. Moreover, in his first novel *Joseph Andrews* (1742), Fielding was again in part responding to what he regarded as the essential immorality of Pamela Andrews. *Joseph Andrews* opens by proposing the case of Pamela's brother who, as a young footman, is constantly assailed sexually by his mistress but manages to retain an unblemished purity. Fielding's novel, of course, goes far beyond this joke (for a counter-attack on a clear case of priggishness by means of an equally glaring one of double-morality does not in itself deserve immortality), and Fielding uses his attack on Richardson, like a similar assault in the first chapter of *Joseph Andrews* on *An Apology for the Life of Colly Cibber*, as a humorous springboard into his fiction. Fielding's charge that Richardson encouraged servant-girls to harbour marital designs on their betters is naturally humorous, but it shows an anxiety for the conservation of society which at root Richardson in fact shared; for the author of *Pamela* had no desire to upset the status quo and, while preserving the social ladder undamaged, would only allow certain privileged persons to rise up it if sufficiently qualified by their virtue, like Pamela, or—one might ill-naturedly conjecture—Samuel Richardson himself.

His second novel *Clarissa* (1747–8) is his masterpiece. Although one of the longest novels in the language, it has a story almost as simple in broad outline as *Pamela*'s. Clarissa Harlowe, the

daughter of a prosperous merchant establishing himself in landed
estates and the status that goes with them, is designed by her
family for an advantageous match with a wealthy man of her own
class, whom she abhors, in order to save her from an aristocratic
suitor, Lovelace, with whom they have quarrelled on the grounds
of his morals and his social superiority. When her parents try to
force her to marry their candidate she resolutely maintains her
'right of refusal', though not of choosing for herself, since she is a
paragon of eighteenth-century virtue. Meanwhile the licentious
and attractive young Lovelace has alarmed her family into applying such cruel pressure on her that, deceived by his false look of
virtue, she willingly flees from them under his protection. After
numerous tricks and escapes, and much resistance on her part,
Lovelace finally imprisons Clarissa in a brothel where he drugs
and rapes her. Too good for this world, she wastes away and,
amidst the lamentations of family and friends, dies confident of a
happy life in heaven, while Lovelace perishes in a duel with one of
her kinsmen, with the words 'LET THIS EXPIATE!' on his lips.

Clarissa was a remarkable book which, with its serious analysis
of the workings of society and the psychological and material
details of life, extended the scope of prose fiction enormously.
Yet this story of injured female innocence and male rapacity shows
the same fundamental pattern of thought as the much cruder
Pamela—a fetishistic devotion to 'purity' in women, set against
an almost demonic sexual drive in the evil man. Lovelace is to a
great degree derived from the libertine character-type in Restoration comedy, though now he is viewed not with indulgence but
with moralistic alarm. The fear of sexuality Richardson's novels
display surely reflects psychologically on him and his contemporary
admirers, and the mystique he attached to virginity was a reflec-
tion of the mechanism by which male society repressed its
women. Fielding, who was won over by the tragic seriousness of
Clarissa, revealed something of his own unconscious, as well as
the complex of thought underlying the novel's sexual morality,
when he reacted to the letter in which Lovelace eventually

announces the rape: 'God forbid that the Man who reads this with dry Eyes should be alone with my Daughter when she hath no Assistance within Call.'

Yet in every respect Richardson's second novel represents an advance over his first. The sexual polarisation central to all his work here produces a tragic conflict which for the first time in English prose fiction connects the individual's moral conduct with his social position and outlook, and with his personal psychology and religious beliefs. In achieving this synthesis Richardson opened up one of the areas which the English novel would explore most insistently for the next two centuries, though few later writers have been able to emulate the simplicity and power of Richardson's tragic movement. For *Clarissa* is not only, like *Pamela*, a deliberately exemplary tale, but also one of the greatest English tragedies.

In the fiercely polarised social and sexual circumstances in which Clarissa finds herself, she is caught between conflicting demands which to her and her author are absolute upon her: the duty of obedience to her family and her need to preserve her own integrity by rejecting the abhorrent suitor. Early on she writes to her confidante, Anna Howe, that Lovelace 'has made things worse for me than before . . . leaving me no other choice, in all appearance, than either to throw myself upon his family, or to be made miserable for ever with Mr. Solmes. But I [am] still resolved to avoid both these evils if possible' (letter 83, Everyman I, pp428–9). But the tragic world will not permit her such an escape, and Richardson cannot devise a solution within his culture to the problem of female identity he has imaginatively posited. Lovelace contrives to build up a false world around her—a world inhabited by creatures of his own making, in which she is surprised to find herself constantly in the wrong. She mistakes the nature of the danger confronting her and falls into his trap. As Lovelace writes to his friend Belford, 'I love, when I dig a pit, to have my prey tumble in with secure feet and open eyes; then a man can look down upon her, with an *O-ho, charmer, how came you there*?' (letter 127, Everyman II, p102). It is not the tragedy of the individual Clarissa alone, for Lovelace eventually falls into his own trap, and the whole world of the novel is transformed by her death and funeral.

The epistolary form enables Richardson to contemplate his action from a number of different moral and social angles corresponding to his various letter-writers, while their letters, 'written, as it were, to the *Moment*', can express their most pressing thoughts and sensations with an immediacy hitherto unequalled in prose. On the one hand the form almost automatically provides moral proportion by juxtaposing the views of the wicked characters with those of carefully established paragons like Anna Howe's suitor, Hickman. On the other, it invites sentiment and the appearance of spontaneous chat and whimsy in the more intimate letters. In this way Richardson is an obvious source of much of the sentimental and self-conscious writing of the later eighteenth century.

After a considerable vogue in England and abroad, and after French masterpieces like Rousseau's *La nouvelle Héloïse* (1760) and Laclos' *Les liaisons dangereuses* (1782), both written under Richardson's influence, the epistolary novel was largely abandoned. It is after all a ponderous form as far as rapid action is concerned, and there is a great deal of redundancy in it. The characters must somehow be made to seem sheer maniacs with the pen, writing letters night and day under the greatest afflictions and managing to dispatch them under the least promising circumstances. In *Sir Charles Grandison* (1753–4), Richardson's third and last novel, the fiction of letter-writing is pushed to its limits, with some letters the length of a good-sized short-story. One of the advantages of the epistolary form, however, is that it offers to overcome the perpetual aesthetic embarrassment as to how a story has got on to the page at all, by presenting the writing as part-and-parcel of the fiction. The novel masquerades as 'fact' with the author posing as the editor of a 'real' collection of letters.

Sir Charles Grandison—to the present-day reader the least

readable of Richardson's three novels—presents, in the author's words, 'the Example of a Man acting uniformly well thro' a Variety of trying Scenes, because all his Actions are regulated by one steady Principle: A Man of Religion and Virtue; of Liveliness and Spirit; accomplished and agreeable; happy in himself, and a Blessing to others' (Preface, OEN, I, p4). The paragon is monstrous, and his female counterpart, Harriet Byron, little better. Richardson's snobbery is at its worst, and smug wisdom, like this from Miss Byron, abounds: 'My grandmamma has observ'd, that young people of small or no fortunes should not be discouraged from marrying . . . The honest poor, as she has often said, are a very valuable part of the creation' (Vol 1, letter 20, OEN, I, p97).

Yet despite all this it is a fascinating book, for in it Richardson introduced subject matter and methods which Jane Austen, Trollope, George Eliot and James would exploit even more effectively, in particular his close analysis of genteel everyday life, with his attention to the speech and gesture of the drawing-room and his ability to present the complex interactions of an assembled company. Most of all in *Grandison* he developed the powerful tool of inter-personal perception as a means of characterisation and as a source of psychological and social action. For example, character A forms an opinion of B on direct perception plus a report from C, or A judges his own conduct by what he thinks he perceives B thinks of it, and so on, through far more complex models. These things are the stock-in-trade of the nineteenth-century novelist, and Richardson's historical importance is that in developing his moral and realistic fiction he opened up vast areas which would prove invaluable to his successors.

HENRY FIELDING

Richardson's great rival, Fielding, wrote in a quite different mode, embodying his comic vision in a highly formalised kind of novel. The laws governing *his* 'new Province of Writing' were ostensibly derived from the Classics and he claimed to accommodate it in the traditional Aristotelian scheme, as comic epic in prose. In doing so, however, he effectively asserted the freedom of this new genre from any previous rules. Like most eighteenth-century writers he justified his fiction by the pragmatic commonplace that it was intended, in the words of the prologue to his play *The Modern Husband* (1731), 'to divert, instruct, and mend mankind'. Since 'Life every where furnishes an accurate Observer with the Ridiculous', Fielding claimed he could derive his improving comedy from 'the vast authentic Book of Nature'. Yet he produced his new fictional worlds by traditional formulas of character and action which are the common property of neo-classical culture.

As a playwright, with over two dozen pieces behind him when he launched into prose fiction with *Joseph Andrews* in 1742, he naturally chose a formalised scheme of characterisation and action. Eighteenth-century comedy throve on character-types and stock situations which can be traced back to the Roman city comedies, and Fielding built his fiction partly by analogy with this inherited system of dramatic decorum. The resulting novels were quite unlike Richardson's. In *Shamela* Fielding had objected to Richardson's superficial morality, but opposing approaches to the aesthetics of fiction were what distinguished the two writers most. In using the epistolary form Richardson tried to conceal as far as possible the facts of composition and pretend that the fiction was not literary artefact at all. With his self-conscious aesthetic approach Fielding took the opposite path. His novels deliberately show signs of formal construction, and moreover he incorporated the otherwise embarrassing fact of composition into his fiction by using a highly self-aware narrative persona, who would not only interpret for the reader the significance of events as they passed, but would stand back from time to time and discuss the whole literary form in which they were cast. In *Tom Jones* the reader is approached directly as a guest at an ordinary or public eating-house, before whom Fielding's narrator as professional host places a feast of delights, pausing at the opening of each of the eighteen books of the novel to discuss literature generally, or some aspect of the bill-of-fare in particular, in a conversational tone which Fielding derives from the urbane manner of essayists like Addison and Steele, who exerted a profound stylistic influence on the English novel for a good 150 years. In the course of the gentlemanly intimacy thus established, the narrator recommends the fiction to the reader as a work of art and nothing else, asserting at the same time, of course, that a self-confessed work of literature can more justly claim moral 'truth' as regards human life than a piece of pretended fact like Richardson's.

In his capacity as literary commentator the narrator expounds a complete theory of fiction, and with all the shifts and indirections that irony can achieve, provides within the work—in *Joseph Andrews* and *Tom Jones*, at least—a complete set of rules by which the fiction should be read. This is not to say that he is unequivocal in this role. He obviously cannot explain how we should interpret his own pronouncements, and so leaves as it were a debate open between himself and the reader. In his other function as interpreter of fictional action the narrator is once more conversational and discursive, and again he is detached from his subject by carefully controlled ironies. Sometimes Fielding's irony is comprehensive and sustained. *Jonathan Wild* (1743) is his longest experiment with the irony of total reversal, and satirises the political career of 'the Great Man', Sir Robert Walpole, through a mock-enthusiastic story of the life of the famous criminal Jonathan Wild, in the character of a 'great man'—making his moral point, as so often, by means of a semantic quibble. Unlike Gay's *The Beggars' Opera* (1728) in which equally sustained irony at Walpole's expense succeeds brilliantly through theatrical spectacle, *Jonathan Wild* tends to become tediously predictable, and the quicksilver surface presented by the ever-shifting ironic stances of *Joseph Andrews* (1742) and *Tom Jones* (1749) is more attractive.

In these great novels the irony serves to reveal true—as

opposed to merely apparent—consistencies in characters and events. For example, when Tom Jones surprises his hypocritical tutor Square in Molly Seagrim's bedroom, the reader is surprised by the sudden revelation, but not by the human possibility of the situation, which the narrator nonetheless playfully insists on explaining as though the reader cannot understand it:

> I question not but the Surprize of the Reader will be here equal to that of *Jones*; as the Suspicions which must arise from the Appearance of this wise and grave Man in such a Place, may seem so inconsistent with that Character, which he hath, doubtless, maintained hitherto, in the Opinion of every one.
>
> (*Tom Jones*, V.v, PEL, pp215–16)

This disingenuous ironic approach enables him to make his moral point more emphatically than would otherwise be permissible: 'But to confess the Truth, this Inconsistency is rather imaginary than real. Philosophers are composed of Flesh and Blood as well as other human Creatures . . .' As usual in Fielding the crucial point is the disparity between a character's theory and practice, and the narrator's explanatory pose is a trick of rhetoric.

Fielding's narrator conceives of a human being in action in life in terms of an actor playing a part on the stage of 'this great Theatre of Nature', with himself as a person privileged to go behind the scenes and examine the human nature that truly underlies the various parts a Garrick may play on different nights. This theatre metaphor for life does not imply that Fielding took human personality to be the product of the roles a person played in life, as Boswell did a few years later, or an existentialist does in our century. On the contrary, like most Augustan humanists he believed in a fundamental, irreducible essence of character which constituted a person's 'true' nature, and which that person's roles in life more or less honestly revealed or wickedly dissembled. So for Fielding psychology was a branch of ethics, and the examination of the springs of human action a profoundly moral activity.

Given such views it is obvious why Fielding subscribed to a doctrine of faith in works in line with current latitudinarian Church of England thought, which maintained that "tis the *Doer* and not the Hearer of the Word of the Lord which shall be blessed', and hence condemned Methodism with its emphasis on the inclination of the soul, as so much hypocritical cant. If faith without works was unacceptable to him, so was moral judgement from actions alone, without regard to motives. Latitudinarianism satisfied him because it lay an equal stress on both components in his moral and comic vision, demanding that an essential faith be acted out in life.

The sermons of the latitudinarian divine Isaac Barrow feature prominently in Fielding's last novel, *Amelia* (1751), where they bring Amelia's erring husband back into the fold, and in his earliest, *Joseph Andrews*, where they are much admired by Abraham Adams, the good parson who, more than Joseph, is the hero of the novel and is, as his name signifies, both an innocent representative of Everyman and an exemplum of faith in works. He can, literally as well as morally, mistake the nature of the world around him, but his is a natural goodness which, Fielding says, cannot be defeated in the end.

Natural goodness is all, and Fielding praised the 'natural' gentleman whose qualities and good deeds sprang from a spontaneous goodness of heart, but not the gentleman who was a gentleman only by virtue of his rank and a superficial polish of manners. Mr Allworthy in *Tom Jones* is a paragon of a gentleman in Fielding's good sense, and Tom himself, though imprudent, turns out to be a 'natural' gentleman too. A heart actuated by a benevolence which is approved by reason determines a good man for Fielding. Hence Tom, beset as he is by females, is not sexually culpable in the same way as his friend Nightingale, who has seduced his landlady's daughter with false promises.

The plot of *Tom Jones* may be said in part to act out a pun on the idea of the 'natural gentleman'. From the first Tom is known to be 'natural' in the sense of illegitimate, but as the story proceeds he seems to Mr Allworthy to lack both the moral and the social qualities of a gentleman. Through his actions and motives he is finally revealed as, morally speaking, a 'natural gentleman', and though still illegitimate is rewarded with social gentility when revealed as Mr Allworthy's bastard nephew.

There are no wholly good characters in Fielding, for even the best, like Mr Allworthy, have minor lapses. The commonplace perception that there are no moral blacks or whites distinguishes Fielding's characterisation from the gross simplicity of the earlier chivalric romances, but he is crude beside the psychologically more acute Richardson. Yet, except in the case of the fine ironies of Jane Austen, the subject of 'mixed characters', neither wholly good nor bad, is approached theoretically in very much Fielding's simplistic terms until these are rendered obsolete by the far subtler moral discriminations of George Eliot and the more delicate psychological apperceptions of Henry James. The origin of this so-called 'realistic' morality and psychology of Fielding's is the Augustan thinker's simultaneous hope and disgust at human nature, but for Fielding the contradictions inherent in human existence are far less violent than for Pope or Swift.

For one thing there is an important element of moral hope in Fielding which softens the Augustan vision, yet he lacks either Defoe's belief in personal amelioration or Richardson's examination of the labyrinthine subtleties of human motives, actions and emotions. Then there is an infusion of that closely allied eighteenth-century phenomenon, sentiment, which can be seen in all the novels, and which damages the final one, *Amelia*, fatally, because it is impossible to use a detached ironic narrator while at the same time displaying an authorial sentimental attachment to a major character. The trouble arises from an inability to deal with a virtuous young female character without producing a mentally non-existent doll-figure, who can be nothing more than a receptacle for the reader's and narrator's sentiment. Nothing can save a stimulating ironic commentary when it is contradicted with insipidities like these.

As regards happy endings *Amelia* is again the worst offender with its overwhelming final dose of *Gemütlichkeit*, but nevertheless Fielding's is not a totally sentimental vision, since there are characters too wicked for moral redemption, while for a true sentimentalist no one is beyond the pale. In Fielding's great novels, *Joseph Andrews* and *Tom Jones*, any sentimental writing is restrained by the overall ironic control, but the intellectual strength which derives from this distancing is lost in *Amelia* because the ironic framework has broken down.

CHAPTER 3

Quixotic and Picaresque Fiction

Fielding's greatest predecessor in ironic narrative was Cervantes, whose *Don Quixote* (1605–15) was more complex in its narrative framework than *Tom Jones* in having not only a fictitious author but a fictitious translator from the Arabic as well. Cervantes's exploitation of the ironic possibilities of third-person narrative was more thorough than Fielding's, because while the former coloured his fiction with doubts as to the nature of literature and the whole basis of human knowledge of the self and of the world, the latter largely confined his irony to suggesting an equivocal relationship between a knowable self and a reality free from ontological uncertainty. In the world of *Don Quixote* it is not possible to be clear as to what is fact and what is imagination; for example, Don Quixote becomes increasingly convinced that there is a writer somewhere recording his exploits, so that the story-teller seems to exist as much in the knight's imagination as vice versa. Fielding's principal addition to Cervantes's kind of episodic novel was a more obvious attention to structure, and the imposition of an epic unity of action as Aristotle defined it, brought about by careful plotting on the model of the sort of drama Fielding himself had written. Nevertheless it is Cervantes who seems more 'modern' when we read him today.

Cervantes influenced English fiction extensively, bequeathing it the idea of an episodic novel built round the humorous adventures of a pair of protagonists who, like the Don Quixote and Sancho Panza of Fielding's Spanish master, have significantly opposed views of the world and everything they encounter in it. Such are Parson Adams and Joseph in *Joseph Andrews*, and Tom and Partridge in *Tom Jones*. Such, too, in the next century, are Mr Pickwick and Sam Weller in *Pickwick Papers* and Martin and Mark Tapley in *Martin Chuzzlewit*, not to mention a host of other twin protagonists. Much of the humour derives from the clash of world views in which a down-to-earth manservant must complement and even preserve his innocent or other-worldly master. But the use of twin protagonists is not an exclusive or sufficient mark of the quixotic mode.

The true mark of the quixotic adventurer is that he puts a false construction on the world about him because his mode of thought is out of joint with his circumstances. For the Knight of the Sorrowful Countenance himself it was romances of chivalry that turned a peasant girl into his lady Dulcinea del Toboso, windmills into giants and a barber's basin into a magic helmet. Unlike *Tom Jones, Joseph Andrews* is quixotic in this sense. Parson Adams is an innocent, constantly surprised by his fellow men because his understanding of humanity is largely drawn from his own good heart and his favourite classical authors. Unlike the world of *Don Quixote*, which is ultimately unknowable, Fielding's world is solid and comprehensible if correctly approached. Parson Adams makes mistakes within a knowable reality, and his kind of natural innocence is continued by Dickens in Mr Pickwick.

The quixotic protagonist and indeed the whole quixotic pattern are seen in their purest English form in Charlotte Lennox's rather neglected but very readable novel *The Female Quixote* (1752). Arabella has been brought up in seclusion from the world and unguided by any experienced older person. Although well educated for her sex, she has been feeding her mind on romances of chivalry by writers like Scudéry and La Calprenède, until her head has been turned and she is unable to understand the real eighteenth-century world she inhabits. She insists on responding to her real-life suitors and friends according to the strictest conventions of courtly love, as though they were characters in romance. Her delusions are finally dispelled by a learned doctor who lectures her roundly in Johnsonian terms on the need to control the imagination by reference to reality. For the next half century the character of the Female Quixote is frequently used to signify a mind deranged by the excesses of romance, and the dangers supposedly inherent in the reading of unrealistic literature.

'The only Excellence of Falsehood,' the Johnsonian doctor tells Arabella, 'is its Resemblance to Truth' (IX.xi, OEN, p378), and this realistic principle runs through all Johnson's criticism. In his prose tale *Rasselas* (1759) the young Prince of Abissinia is warned that the unrestrained operation of fantasy leads to 'disorders of the intellect' (chapter 44, OEN, p113). Humanistic reason and stoical endurance in the presence of God and of a definable but hard reality are the virtues Johnson teaches, and the literature which is to serve this end must be faithful to the general truths of 'nature' as interpreted by the Augustans. This did not mean that he approved of Fielding, for all the latter's concern with fidelity to human nature. In his important *Rambler* essay number 4 on prose fiction, Johnson claimed that mixed characters were dangerous examples for 'the Young, the Ignorant, and the Idle' for whom novels served 'as Lectures of Conduct, and Introductions into Life', because if 'good and bad Qualities' were mingled in the 'principal Personages' the reader might 'lose the Abhorrence of their Faults . . . or, perhaps, regard them with some Kindness for being united with so much Merit'. That 'vicious' book *Tom Jones* was his main unnamed target in this essay. He regularly depreciated Fielding, and correspondingly praised Richardson for having 'enlarged the Knowledge of human Nature, and taught the Passions to move at the Command of Virtue'.

The Female Quixote concerns a departure from an Augustan

norm of reason, and is a world away from Cervantes in as much as Arabella's delusions throw no doubt on reality, being acted out against the secure world of Johnsonian commonsense. In this respect the novel resembles Jane Austen's only exercise in the quixotic in *Northanger Abbey* (written 1798–9) where Catherine Morland, deluded by an overdose of Gothic romances such as Mrs Radcliffe's *The Mysteries of Udolpho*, concludes that her widowed host General Tilney is concealing the murder of his wife. She is brought to see that England at the end of the eighteenth century is not a country in which the terrors of Gothic mystery actually prevail, and a more-or-less Johnsonian mental self-control is re-established. Catherine's quixotic delusions are not only a very successful joke at literary fashions, but serve as a metaphor for the loss of that reasonable control over the mind which in the opinion of a Jane Austen or a Samuel Johnson should be sustained by constant reference to external reality. It is possible to see the limits of pure quixoticism in this kind of novel by noting two other non-quixotic types of mistake which Catherine Morland makes in *Northanger Abbey*, and which are more characteristic of Jane Austen's fiction as a whole. One is the important plot-generating device whereby one character is for a long time in suspense as to another's feelings because circumstances and the *convenances* forbid their open expression, as in the case of Catherine and Henry Tilney. The other is the serious misestimate of another person's character, like Catherine's misjudgement of Isabella's. Both of these are the very staple of English realistic fiction. Neither is quixotic, but for a writer relying on a commonsensical realistic framework both are probably susceptible of more novelistic exploitation than the quixotic state of not knowing in what world one is.

There is another line in English fiction which derives from *Don Quixote*; but, whereas the modification of the quixotic in Lennox and Austen is the logical result of historical and philosophical reorientations, this other pseudo-quixotic line shows a thorough misunderstanding of the original and debases Don

Quixote into an eccentric do-gooder who knocks around the world righting real or imaginary wrongs. Such in part is Mr Pickwick, but the most glaring example of the simplified quixote is the hero of *Sir Launcelot Greaves* (1760–1) by Tobias Smollett, one of the novelists who most influenced Dickens. Having just completed a crude translation of *Don Quixote*, Smollett rushed out his own English quixote who absurdly rides round mid-eighteenth-century England in armour with his English Sancho Panza, Timothy Crabshaw, relieving maidens and others in distress. The Knight of the Sorrowful Countenance has been transmogrified into a handsome, wealthy young baronet, who displays excellent impulses but inexplicable behaviour in a series of good scenes which arise from the hero's determination 'to remedy evils which the law cannot reach'. After exposing an evil magistrate, witnessing an election which shows Smollett at his Hogarthian best, and spending time in a prison and a madhouse, Sir Launcelot reaps Smollett's usual reward of an insipid beauty, and returns to his ancestral estates to a chorus of loving tenants and lots of rustic jollity.

In the course of his career Smollett experimented with most of the narrative modes then available to him, and is rightly less known as a failed quixotic writer than as our foremost exponent of a type of picaresque or rogue literature. But his picaresque, too, is remote from the Spanish novels which founded the tradition. Quixotic and picaresque fiction are originally quite distinct, and it is only since the eighteenth century adapted both to its own taste that there could be thought to be any connexion between the two. The term 'picaresque' is often loosely applied, but it should strictly refer to the fictional lives of delinquents ('*pícaros*' in Spanish), criminal self-seekers, thieves and murderers, be-trayers of their closest associates and traitors to their benefactors. (Defoe uses the English 'picaroon' to mean a pirate-ship.) In its true sense the picaresque does not concern the adventures of the good-hearted traveller through the world, though the term was soon stretched to cover imperfect heroes like those of Lesage's

Gil Blas (1715–35) in France or Smollett's *Roderick Random* (1748) in Britain. The word has often been outrageously misused with reference to any episodic fiction, including even such archetypes of literary innocence as *The Vicar of Wakefield* and *Huckleberry Finn*. Worse still, *Don Quixote* has been dubbed picaresque; but the Knight of the Sorrowful Countenance is no criminal, nor is there anything picaresque about his delusions.

The confusion arose because of a few superficial connexions between quixotic and picaresque fiction. Both are episodic in form and both first flourished in Spain at the beginning of the 1600s: the two parts of the most influential picaresque novel, *Guzmán de Alfarache*, were published in 1599 and 1604, and those of *Don Quixote* in 1605 and 1615, while their authors were exact contemporaries. Finally in a very broad sense both are realistic and anti-romantic. Mateo Alemán's *Guzmán* was part of a movement towards a serious realistic treatment of the world which was intended to convey a moral vision in a way inconceivable in the high-flown irrelevance of the chivalric romances then popular. And, of course, the falseness of romance was Cervantes's chief target in *Don Quixote*. Both these kinds of fiction are satirical, but picaresque satire is bitter while, for all its almost tragic sadness as well as humour, the quixotic displays none of the *pícaro*'s deep disgust at human existence. Moreover, their fictional methods are quite different. A picaresque novel is typically told in the first person, and the narrator achieves a moral perspective by interspersing his narrative with moral reflections. In genuine quixotic fiction, on the other hand, moral judgement, like humour, arises from the refraction of the hero's deeds and delusions through an ironic third-person narrative, which in the case of Cervantes and Fielding is controlled by a fictionalised author-narrator.

The typical protagonist of the Spanish picaresque novel, as seen in the person of Alemán's Guzmán, is a bastard whose origins are emblematic of the corruption of fallen man. He wilfully abandons what home security he has, and sets out on a career of delinquency which takes him through extremes of comfort and beggary. As he passes through different strata of society in the course of his life of crime, he can display, moralise upon and bitterly rail against the sick condition of the fallen world. Finally, misfortune—prison or the galleys—brings him to repentance and he sees the possibility of redemption. The motive force of picaresque satire is a bitter belief that there is a gulf set between the perfection of grace and the rotten state of the actual world.

Picaresque fiction was enormously popular throughout seventeenth-century Europe. In England, for example, James Mabbe's *The Rogue* (1623), a translation of Alemán's *Guzmán*, ran through many editions before the end of the century, and there were numerous imitations of the Spanish originals in various languages, including *The English Rogue* (1665–71), in which sheer sensationalism predominates over other literary qualities. The picaresque shows itself in two main areas in eighteenth-century English fiction: the novels of Defoe, and the different kind of episodic first-person form which Smollett acquired for his *Roderick Random* from his favourite French novelist Lesage, whose *Gil Blas* was itself an adaptation of the methods of *Guzmán* to the politer world of early eighteenth-century France.

More than any other major English writer, Defoe can be called a picaresque novelist. As a popular biographer of notorious criminals he may have found that fictional criminal autobiography came easily to his energetic pen, especially with the precedent of Bunyan's *The Life and Death of Mr Badman* (1680) behind him, though in terms of fictional method Defoe is closer to the Spanish picaresque novel than to any other previous literature, putting a familiar form to a different, distinctively modern use.

We saw earlier how both a novel like *Guzmán* and one of Defoe's presented problems of consistency of narrative tone because in each case the protagonist recounted his life 'with a tone in which glee and compunction alternately predominated'. Like Guzmán, Defoe's narrators have repented after their delinquent careers, but the interpretation Defoe puts on their lives is new. In the first place Defoe is less theological and more sociological. For him it is less a symbol of corruption than an observable fact that uncared-for illegitimate children like Colonel Jack are brought up to crime, and that social pressure—or 'necessity', in his language—can turn more fortunate people to whoring and thieving too. Then again in the Spanish novel it is inherently wicked to change one's role in life and contradict the order of things by creating oneself anew, since as Mabbe's Guzmán says, 'selfe-confidence causeth a forgetfulnesse of God'. Things look quite different to Defoe, the English protestant tradesman, for whom individual social advancement is a right and is good. Whatever a Defoe character may repent at the end of his life, any upward mobility into or within the 'middle station of life' is not part of it.

The acquisition of wealth is no longer essentially wicked either to the mercantile capitalist. Between *Guzmán* and *Moll Flanders* the image of money has changed from the medieval and renaissance vision of a golden temptation to the deadly sin of avarice, into a highly practical means of trading and buying things—including status. It is no longer a yellow heap to gloat over but currency or a bill of exchange, to be coveted, of course, but to be used for some practical purpose in a recognisably modern market situation. Defoe alone in his day shows a modern attitude to economics, and we must wait until the Victorian age before the old-style morality view of money is once again so completely replaced in literature by this realistic approach. In general Defoe's fiction retains in a highly patterned form the older plan of error and repentance, and his detail is emblematic, as well as insistently realistic. His novels, however, are not satire at the expense of the world, like the original picaresque literature, but show the attempt of the puritan conscience to reconcile material and spiritual prosperity in life.

The other derivative of the picaresque tradition in eighteenth-century French and English fiction was very different—still satirical, but stripped of its religious perspective altogether. To conform to current taste it contracted the moral horizons of picaresque satire, which were cosmic and eternal in *Guzmán*, by discarding the narrator's religious commentary: Lesage, for example, published a French translation of *Guzmán* (1732) 'purged of superfluous moralising'. In order to get the eighteenth-century reader's sympathy for the protagonist, Lesage's own novel *Gil Blas* turns him from a criminal into a quite amiable adventurer, as much sinned against as sinning, who from humble origins eventually achieves a social position and prosperity by his resourceful opportunism. This is probably the earliest novel to deal with the progressive education of the hero on his way through the world. Gil Blas first learns practical wisdom, and is finally cured of avarice and ambition by imprisonment and a fever, so that he can be rewarded at the end with a country estate where he may live free from the corruption of the world that has been satirised throughout. True picaresque delinquency is detached from Gil Blas himself and incorporated in inset narratives, leaving the hero himself as an averagely weak character, susceptible to temptation and a bit cowardly, and surrounded by vice on every side. With his strengths and his failings he is a satisfactorily complex character for the hero of a realistic work and may be seen as the prototype of many modern anti-heroes.

TOBIAS SMOLLETT

Smollett not only translated *Gil Blas* (1747–8) but consciously 'modelled' his first novel *Roderick Random* on it. Though far from perfect, Random is even more a victim than Gil Blas, and Smollett's stated aim is to arouse 'that generous indignation which ought to animate the reader against the sordid and vicious disposition of the world' by representing 'modest merit struggling with every difficulty to which a friendless orphan is exposed' (Preface, Everyman, pp3–5).

Smollett is our first important novelist to incorporate a significant amount of autobiographical material into a novel. The general pattern in *Random* of the supposed orphan who passes through hardships and destitution to reach prosperity, discover his father and marry the beautiful girl, is not drawn from the novelist's own life at a factual level (though it may well cast light on his psychology). But Roderick's time at Glasgow University, his medical training, and the brilliant scenes of his naval service as a surgeon's mate, all draw on Smollett's own experience, while the cruel treatment of the writer Mr Melopoyn at the hands of theatre managers and patrons is a bitter account of Smollett's attempts to get his tragedy *The Regicides* performed. The names are changed but the story is otherwise factual except as regards the quality of the rejected play-script. The early development of prose fiction shows the progressive exploitation of larger and larger areas of life in the novel and, although Smollett was less penetrating about society and social relations than Defoe or Richardson, he also importantly extended the area in which fiction could confidently operate.

Roderick is no *pícaro*, but the victim of 'the iniquity of mankind' (chapter 21, Everyman, p119) who, on looking back on his past 'crimes', 'found them so few and venial, that I could not comprehend the justice of that Providence, which . . . left me a prey to famine' (chapter 43, Everyman, p242). Near the end of his adventures he is told 'that although some situations of my life had been low, yet none of them had been infamous; that my indigence had been the crime not of me, but of fortune . . .' (chapter 56, Everyman, p338). He is a morally passive character who claims no great virtue, and rejects crime largely out of disgust at 'the infamy that attends detection' (chapter 60, Everyman, p364). The dominant theme is now worldly education through experience, which 'enlarged the understanding, improved the heart, steeled the constitution, and qualified a young man for all the duties and enjoyments of life, much better than any education which affluence could bestow' (chapter 66, Everyman, p408).

Step by step the original religious perspective of picaresque fiction has been replaced by the more worldly concern of character-formation in the hero. There are still scenes from low-life, and the protagonist still changes his character with his clothes (chapter 44, Everyman, p255), but now he eventually finds himself (as it were) in fortune and marriage. Endings are always unsatisfactory in Smollett. Most of this novel presents Roderick's defeat by the world, and an implausible bit of plot is worked in to recompense him for his sufferings, in defiance of probability, the morality of the day and every other consideration except wish fulfilment. The original picaresque protagonist found eventual happiness in the anticipation of grace. Smollett secularised the reward and presented the heaven-on-earth of a philoprogenitive marriage as a substitute, just as many Victorian novelists were to do.

Whatever his weaknesses, Smollett never wholly repeats himself. In *Peregrine Pickle* (1751) he switches to third-person narrative (probably under the influence of *Tom Jones*) and in doing so loses the distinctive picaresque quality of fictional autobiography. The novel follows Lesage's plan of chastening its immoral protagonist by taking him through a variety of scenes of fortune and misfortune, and contact with vice in high and low places. This is not finely structured art, like Fielding's, but in his pursuit of an unidealised view of the world Smollett has developed his own kind of episodic fiction. Although not a novelist or an innovator of the stature of Richardson or Fielding, Smollett did as much as any other writer to test out a whole range of fictional possibilities for later writers to choose from. In *Peregrine Pickle* and *Sir Launcelot Greaves*, for example, he makes use of a quite unselfconscious narrator, who suffers no aesthetic embarrassment at the existence of his tale and feels no need to explain its presence on the page. Much nineteenth-century fiction has Smollett's example as a precedent for its straightforward narrative method, rather than the highly self-aware narrator of *Tom Jones*.

Roderick Random and *Peregrine Pickle* show up the strengths and weaknesses of the episodic method. The lack of a controlling plot-line is damaging, except in those parts of *Roderick Random* where the hero's personality and fate are sufficiently interesting to form a coherent centre. The advantage of episodic narrative, of course, lay in the ease with which a variety of social settings could be used to present a 'balanced' view of the virtues and vices of mankind. But satire in these novels is largely confined to episodes rather than integrated into one total satiric vision. Besides, the desire to make each incident a vivid self-contained unit frequently brought out a limited and crude type of comedy based on the practical joke. Smollett's comedy is unlike Fielding's, which depends on a tight, almost dramatic plot, but even at his loosest Smollett can produce vivid vignettes of 'humours' characters, some of the most interesting being those who speak and behave largely in terms of their occupations, such as sailors who remain sailors when on land. Captain Crowe in *Sir Launcelot Greaves* is here recounting an accident at sea:

> —ship deep laden—rich cargo—current setting into the bay—hard gale—lee shore—all hands in the boat—tow round the headland—self pulling for dear blood, against the whole crew—Snap go the finger-braces—crack went the eye-blocks. Bounce daylight—flash starlight—down I foundered, dark as hell—whizz went my ears, and my head spun like a whirligig.
>
> (chapter 2)

This method of characterisation in which the character is presented in terms of the linguistic space he occupies was one of Smollett's innovations that most appealed to Dickens, who, with his even greater stylistic inventiveness, carried these effects so much farther that he could project a character's complete world-picture in a few economical utterances.

In his own day Smollett was attacked for describing people with all their natural imperfections, instead of holding up models for emulation as Richardson did in *Clarissa* and *Sir Charles Grandison*. Samuel Johnson, for one, considered it particularly dangerous to mingle good and bad qualities in a sympathetic character. *Ferdinand, Count Fathom* (1753) can be seen as Smollett's attempt to meet such objections, and to unite nature 'warts and all' with impeccable morality, by presenting two parallel protagonists—an out-and-out villain of a picaresque type in contrast with a model of virtue. The novel unfortunately falls to pieces because of this, but is historically one of his most interesting as it exemplifies a gross simplification of moral problems, which is increasingly common later in the century, and involves a polarisation between a rather sentimental and bloodless virtue and an almost demonic villainy.

Smollett's experiments continued with his pseudo-quixotic *Sir Launcelot Greaves*, and ended with *Humphry Clinker* (1771), a satirical novel in epistolary form in which a humane but crusty old Tory squire, Matthew Bramble, tours the country with a varied party who all react to what they see in their own way, so that although there is very little plot a complex satirical vision of the Britain of the day is built up from the juxtaposition of letters from Bramble himself, his mean and methodistical sister Tabitha, her servant Winifred Jenkins, and Bramble's young niece and varsity nephew. *Humphry Clinker* contains by far his most fascinating and controlled satire, but in terms of story it is weak, and in method the least forward-looking of all his novels. Historically Smollett's achievement is best seen as experiment and not accomplishment; although not of the stature of Richardson and Fielding, he made as great a contribution as they did to opening up the possibilities of English prose fiction.

CHAPTER 4

Sterne, Sentiment and its Opponents

Despite the technical variety and the personal and ethical differences which divided the mid-eighteenth-century novelists so far discussed, their similarities were no less significant. Basically they all believed in the adequacy of literature to give an account of the world, on the basis of a general understanding of 'human nature' exemplified in particular cases, assuming as they did that a literary representation of the world could be true (within the limits of human fallibility) because of the validity of the moral generalisations on which it was based.

LAURENCE STERNE

It was largely in reaction to this position that in 1759 Laurence Sterne published the first part of his great anti-novel, *The Life and Opinions of Tristram Shandy, Gentleman*, which by sophisticated play with the techniques of the conventional novel-forms sought to cast doubt on these humanistic assumptions concerning the place of literature at the centre of western civilisation.

Both Richardson and Fielding were conscious literary innovators, and both claimed the right to lay down for themselves the rules of their own respective species of composition. Sterne's procedure in *Tristram Shandy* (1759–67) was to take the characteristics and problems of these new forms and push them to the point of paradox. So, taking an idea like Fielding's theory of the comic epic in prose as his butt, Tristram Shandy explains that he is not following classical authorities, such as Horace, 'for in writing what I have set about, I shall confine myself neither to his rules, nor to any man's rules that ever lived' (I.iv, PEL, p38).

Tristram Shandy, the *reductio ad absurdum* of self-conscious narrative, turns out to be quite as much about itself and the process of its own composition as anything else. Sterne's starting points here are Fielding's fictionalised author-narrator of *Tom Jones* and some of Richardson's correspondents, such as Lovelace in *Clarissa*, who is particularly conscious of the 'moment' of composition when writing about his paradoxical feelings for the heroine, and often vividly—and facetiously—fictionalises his physical and mental movements as he writes:

> Limbs, why thus convulsed! Knees, till now so firmly knit, why thus relaxed? Why beat ye thus together? Will not these trembling fingers, which twice have refused to direct the pen, fail me in the arduous moment? . . . This project is not to end in *matrimony*, surely?
>
> (letter 224, Everyman II, p499)

In their different ways, both Richardson and Fielding experimented with the use of self-conscious narrators, and while Smollett largely proceeded by ignoring the aesthetic and philosophical problems presented by an awareness by the narrative of its own existence on the page, Sterne went to the opposite extreme and wrote one of the funniest books in the language principally about these very problems.

Sterne achieves this high degree of self-awareness in his narrative by a thorough fictionalisation of his narrator in the role of author:

> It is not half an hour ago, when (in the great hurry and precipitation of a poor devil's writing for daily bread) I threw a fair sheet, which I had just finished, and carefully wrote out, slap into the fire, instead of the foul one.

46

> Instantly I snatched off my wig, and threw it perpendicularly,
> with all imaginable violence, up to the top of the room . . . but
> there was an end of the matter; nor do I think any thing else in
> Nature, would have given such immediate ease . . .
>
> (IV.xvii, PEL, pp291–2)

To complete the system the reader too must be brought into the
book as 'Sir' or 'Madam' as the occasion requires, and addressed,
as in *Tom Jones* though far more intimately, in terms of a 'slight
acquaintance' destined to 'grow into familiarity' and 'terminate
in friendship' (I.vi, PEL, p41): for, Tristram Shandy explains,
'Writing, when properly managed, (as you may be sure I think
mine is) is but a different name for conversation' (II.xi, PEL, p127).
Moreover the reader is not meant to remain a passive partner in
his relationship with the author and at one stage is given a blank
page in which to fill in his own ideal of the most 'concupiscible'
woman in the world to serve in place of a description of widow
Wadman (VI.xxxviii, PEL, pp450–1).

The whimsical tone and conversational intimacy are matched
by a contrived disorder, ostensibly the result of Tristram's 'most
religious' method—'for I begin with writing the first sentence—
and trusting to Almighty God for the second' (VIII.ii, PEL, p516).
Sterne constructs his narrative according to a psychological
rather than a logical plan, by applying to Tristram Shandy's
mental workings Locke's concept of the association of ideas,
whereby

> *ideas*, that in themselves are not at all of kin, come to be so united
> in some men's minds that it is very hard to separate them, they
> always keep in company, and the one no sooner at any time comes
> into the understanding but its associate appears with it . . .
>
> (*An Essay Concerning Human Understanding*, II.xxxiii.5)

Tristram is using Locke's terms when he speaks of a curious
'chain of ideas' which has led him apparently irrelevantly to 'the
affair of *Whiskers*' (V.i, PEL, p340). Lockian psychology is rich in
explanations for individual and eccentric mental behaviour, and

for Sterne nothing in the working of the individual mind is irrelevant. General truths take second place to idiosyncrasy. As regards narrative order, this all implies that if a story-teller is 'a man of the least spirit' he cannot possibly

> drive on his history, as a muleteer drives on his mule,—straight forward;—for instance, from Rome all the way to Loretto, without ever once turning his head aside either to the right hand or to the left . . .
>
> (I.xiv, PEL, p64)

The occasion of this last statement is that Tristram feels the need to describe at length the conditions of his mother's marriage settlement before he can fully explain how he came to be born in the country; and in general in Shandean narrative it is impossible to understand the present until all anterior circumstances have been cleared up. The process turns out to be never-ending: Sterne has made his point that literature can never give a total explanation of anything.

The need to go back and explain all the facts which bear on the present story and on the minds, however idiosyncratic, of the participants means that, although the book's title is *The Life and Opinions of Tristram Shandy* and although it begins with Tristram's conception, he is not in fact born until a quarter of the way through and his life is hardly mentioned for long stretches thereafter. Eventually, after hundreds of pages, having started nine months before his birth, the book ends four whole years before it.

Tristram Shandy not only follows the turns of its supposed author's mind but must be equally faithful to those of the other characters and follow all their mental hobby-horses too. Again Locke's association of ideas provides the explanation for eccentric mental habits and obsessions:

> There is scarce anyone that does not observe something that seems odd to him, and is in itself really extravagant, in the opinions, reasonings, and actions of other men . . . [T]here is scarce a man so free from it but that, if he should always on all occasions argue or

do as in some cases he constantly does, would not be thought fitter for Bedlam than civil conversation.

(II.xxxiii. 1 and 4)

Tristram's father and Uncle Toby display the extremes of 'hobby-horsical' reasoning, one largely in the realm of obscure scholarship (giving Sterne the opportunity for wonderful learned wit in the Rabelaisean tradition), the other interpreting everything he hears in terms of military science, being a wounded veteran of the Irish and French wars of 1689–97, obsessively acting out in miniature on his bowling-green the sieges of the campaigns of 1702–13. If the mind worked like this, Sterne was saying, then clearly no simple description of a person's character could provide an adequate explanation of behaviour which, like the 'infinitude of oddities' in Tristram's father, 'baffled, Sir, all calculations' (V.xxiv, PEL, pp374–5). Despite all an author's digressive efforts to trace the mind's peculiarities, the self is ultimately unknowable, as Tristram again acknowledges:

—My good friend, quoth I—as sure as I am I—and you are you—
—And who are you? said he. —Don't puzzle me; said I.

(VII.xxxiiii, PEL, p500)

The result is that the commonsensical world of Augustan certainty is destroyed. Hence Dr Johnson's curt dismissal of Sterne as 'odd', and the distrust of later thinkers too, for whom human nature must be comprehensible if sense is to be made of our world.

One of the corollaries to Lockian association is that our experience of duration is not a matter of clock time, but depends upon the succession of ideas in our minds. When waiting for Tristram's birth his father rhetorically exclaims that two hours and ten minutes have passed, 'and I know not how it happens, brother Toby,—but to my imagination it seems almost an age'. He is preparing to explain it in Lockian terms when Uncle Toby most uncharacteristically forestalls him with ' 'Tis owing, entirely ... to the succession of our ideas' (III.xviii, PEL, p199), leaving his exasperated brother only the details of the theory to fill in. Clock time is the great enemy in *Tristram Shandy*, and Tristram's father wishes 'there was not a clock in the kingdom' (III.xviii, PEL, p200) because of the blow dealt him by his wife on the first page, on the night of Tristram's conception, when she unseasonably asked him, '*Pray, my dear . . . have you not forgot to wind up the clock?*'—a question which arises only because of the arbitrary Lockian association in her and her husband's minds of sex with winding the clock, since he performs both household duties on the first Sunday of each month.

From the very beginning, time is one of the chief protagonists, and the seeming chaos of the book can be seen to be organised round a number of different time-schemes, the orderly time-flow of the conventional autobiography, however, being lost in the process. A good proportion of the events take place years before Tristram's birth in 1718. Uncle Toby, for example, was wounded at the siege of Namur in 1695, and has thereafter lived much of his life vicariously as he acts out the sieges of the wars of 1702–13 up to the demolition of Dunkirk, living two lives simultaneously —the one in and around Shandy Hall and synchronous with his neighbours', and the other in his imagination on the Continent, and divided from the former by the time taken for the military news to arrive. The second sometimes threatens to take over completely, as it does when he plans with Corporal Trim his miniature demolition of Dunkirk:

> . . . we'll demolish the mole,—next fill up the harbour,—then retire into the citadel, and blow it up into the air: and having done that, corporal, we'll embark for England.—We are there, quoth the corporal, recollecting himself—Very true, said my uncle Toby —looking at the church.
>
> (VI.xxxiv, PEL, p447)

This dual existence is lost to him with the Treaty of Utrecht of 1713, and with it one of his chronologies:

No more could my uncle Toby, after passing the French lines, as

he eat his egg at supper, from thence break into the heart of
France . . . march up to the gates of Paris, and fall asleep with
nothing but ideas of glory . . .

(VI.xxxv, PEL, p447)

On top of such chronological complexities within the events
Tristram Shandy is purveying to us, he superimposes an awareness of not only the moment of writing but the length of time
taken to write certain books or chapters, and even the average
time taken to read them as well. Because of his need to account
for everything and every moment, he involves himself in in-
extricable difficulties, which demonstrate the impossibility of his
task, and by extension, the limitations of literature too:

> I am this month one whole year older than I was this time twelve-
> month; and having got, as you perceive, almost into the middle of
> my fourth volume—and no further than to my first day's life—
> 'tis demonstrative that I have three hundred and sixty-four days
> more life to write just now, than when I first set out; so that in-
> stead of advancing, as a common writer, in my work . . . I am
> just thrown so many volumes back . . .
>
> (IV.xiii, PEL, p286)

Eventually the onward march of clock-time becomes so pressing
on the fictional author that he sets off travelling through France
and Italy, in a flight from death. But, even with a stress on an
apparent 'present', the chronology of the narrative is far from
straightforward. Tristram sometimes has as many as three levels
of awareness of time: the moment of writing, the recent past of
which he is narrating the events, and a more distant past which is
associated with them:

> I am this moment walking across the market-place of Auxerre
> with my father and my uncle Toby . . . and I am this moment also
> entering Lyons with my post-chaise broke into a thousand pieces
> —and I am moreover this moment in a handsome pavillion built
> by Pringello . . . where I now sit rhapsodizing all these affairs.
>
> (VII.xxviii, PEL, p492)

In any past-tense narrative a moment in the past may be meant to be experienced by the reader as a quasi-present, as the past is 'performed', as it were, in the act of reading. So it is possible for Tristram Shandy to write in the past tense of the events of 'to-morrow morning', in a passage in which narrative time and reading time are wilfully confused in a panic-stricken summary of catastrophes:

> . . . a cow broke in (to-morrow morning) to my uncle Toby's fortifications, and eat up two ratio and half of dried grass . . .— Trim insists upon being tried by a court-martial,—the cow to be shot . . . I want swaddling,—but there is no time to be lost in exclamations.—I have left my father lying across his bed, and my uncle Toby in his old fringed chair . . . and promised I would go back to them in half an hour, and five-and-thirty minutes are lapsed already.
>
> (III.xxxviii, PEL, p240)

Most of the tricks Sterne plays are based like this, on paradoxes inherent in much conventional story-telling, and carry to extremes the possibilities and the limitations of fictional narrative.

There was an extraordinary international vogue for Sterne's works, with streams of translations, imitations and spurious continuations still appearing as late as the first years of the next century; what most captivated this European public was not his humour, burlesque and parody but his sentiment. Scenes in *Tristram Shandy* like Le Fever's death, Uncle Toby sparing the life of a fly, or poor, mad, lovelorn Maria, and her goat, drew copious tears, while his *Sentimental Journey* (1768) was the best and most influential novel of the time to be based on the idea of sensibility, or the sympathetic emotional response to the smallest stimuli of joy and sorrow.

SENTIMENTAL WRITING

Until about 1760 the word 'sentimental' largely corresponded to the older use of 'sentiment' as thought, opinion, or moral and religious reflexion, but under the influence of Sterne reason retreated, or was placed under the command of emotion, for, as the hero's father says in Henry Brooke's *The Fool of Quality* (1766–70), 'the understanding cannot reject what the heart so sensibly feels'. Sentimental writers discarded Fielding's carefully balanced ethical scheme whereby virtue is shown in feeling *and* rationally responding to the needs of others, and Richardson's insistence that the emotions be only indulged within a framework of rational morality, duty and principle, although the later sections of Richardson's *Clarissa* remained an important source of sentimental style, with its heavy rhythms, exaggerated diction, religiosity, and lightly veiled sexuality. Writers like Sterne, Henry Brooke and Henry Mackenzie, author of *The Man of Feeling* (1771), returned to Shaftesbury's notion that virtue is inherent in every person, and a '[s]ense of right and wrong . . . a first principle in our constitution', but perverted his position by making sensibility and inclination supplant the rational restraints by which he insisted we must be governed.

The concentration on individual responses which underlies *Tristram Shandy* is the necessary pre-condition for sentiment too. Spasms of feeling, however slight, are better guides to human character than carefully weighed actions, because spontaneous movements of virtue spring from the heart which retains a small portion of prelapsarian goodness. Sentiment enables men to share with God the joys of his creation, even though grief and suffering are ultimately the source of most sentimental satisfaction:

> There is surely . . . a species of pleasure in grief, a kind of soothing and deep delight, that arises with the tears which are pushed from the fountain of God in the soul, from the charities and sensibilities of the human heart divine.
>
> (Henry Brooke, *The Fool of Quality*, 1766, chapter 14, 1859 edition, Vol I, p343)

Charity is dispensed as much for the satisfaction of the giver as the receiver, and promises redemption too. John Wesley found such a second-rate novel as *The Fool of Quality* 'one of the most beautiful pictures that ever was drawn in the world' and, with a number of cuts, turned it into a methodist tract. As late as 1859 Charles Kingsley still thought it would help to make its reader 'a Man, a Christian, and a Gentleman'. But sentiment in general treated religion more as a trigger for fine feelings and tears than as a theological structure of belief, and religious words are frequently transferred from their original uses to heighten the effects of secular descriptions.

Sexuality was subject to similar displacement. In *A Sentimental Journey* Sterne deliberately played up the sexual aspects of sentiment, but some of his contemporaries seem to have overlooked the implications of the enthusiasms, caresses, pantings and flutterings they described so lavishly, while necrophilia was commonplace, from the men who pressed close to Clarissa's coffin in Richardson, to the admirable Mr Clinto in *The Fool of Quality* who slept nine nights in the embrace of his wife's corpse (I, p343). But then sentimental death is different, especially in a book where a virgin's body does not decay because of her purity, or a bereaved mother on the death of her children is happy to have made 'two safe and certain angels' (II, p266; I, pp329–30). Sensitive spirits like Harley, the hero of Mackenzie's *Man of Feeling*, actually expire when they discover they are beloved. Mackenzie's is the most delicate world of sensibility, in which even a press-gang weep as they carry off their man.

In *The Man of Feeling* and much other sentimental literature there is a mixture of satire on a corrupt world and a sanguine view of man's natural goodness. Oliver Goldsmith's *Vicar of Wakefield* (1766) is constructed around just this unresolved conflict between satire of the world through the device of an innocent protagonist who cannot recognise vice beneath a fair exterior, and sentimental approval of this protagonist even in his folly. He is both defeated by the world *and* has his reward, being saved by an arbitrary manipulation of the plot, after passive virtue has been shown to be insufficient. In *The Fool of Quality* Brooke tries to preserve natural goodness by attributing all human evil to upbringing and environment, but has problems reconciling this view with orthodox theology.

The Fool of Quality exposes a whole complex of ideas and feelings involved in late eighteenth-century sentiment, and shows why these are in a way continuous with certain aspects of Victorianism. As the story of the education of the perfect aristocrat by the perfect merchant-prince, *The Fool of Quality* is an allegory of bourgeois ascendancy, showing unbounded confidence in the protestant, capitalist ideology which had triumphed in the revolution of 1688. It consists of a set of exemplary tales of charity and right conduct which show the millionaire merchant to be 'greater than any prince or emperor upon earth' (II, p174), in a world where work and property are morally improving, and where capital investment, by setting even little children to work, can be reckoned 'the greatest of charities, a charity to Great Britain, a charity to mankind' (II, pp178–86). The 'incomparable beauties of the Britannic constitution' (II, p46) rest on every man's God-given right to 'life, liberty, and strength to acquire property', which right is 'natural, inheritable, and indefeasible ... universal, invariable, and inalienable' (II, pp32–3). Those who use their gifts and money for the improvement of themselves and of others earn the name of gentleman—'this supreme of denominations'—indicating moral qualities which have been celebrated since the time of Homer and the Old Testament (I, pp263–9). The process of redefining the concept of gentility to fit middle-class morality rather than aristocratic birth is dear to many Victorian novelists, too, such as Thackeray and Trollope, and in more ways than one Brooke reminds us that what we regard as Victorianism has its roots deep in the eighteenth century. One might be forgiven for misdating 'Remember fair play and Old England!' by the better part of a century (I, p262). Dickens was deeply influenced by the domestic sentiment of *The Vicar of Wakefield*, and the vicar's assertion that in the 'middle order of mankind are generally to be found all the arts, wisdom, and virtues of society' (chapter 19, OEN, p97) perfectly illustrates a continuous and developing tradition of bourgeois thought from Defoe to its final triumph in the nineteenth century.

The question of charity, which is closely bound up with all these social attitudes, forms a subject of unprecedented concern in novels of the later eighteenth century. The willingness of the well-to-do to relieve the unfortunate is an essential part of sentiment, but is a moral touchstone, too, in the fiction of writers like Fanny Burney and Maria Edgeworth, who reject the extravagances of sentiment in favour of reason and self-control. In Burney's novels charity shows a humane and rational desire to reduce distress, but the afflictions which bring people to misery are regarded as a natural and inevitable part of human existence, so that nothing can really be done to eliminate the most frequent sorts of suffering. Moreover this charity does not disturb the *status quo* since help must be carefully adjusted to the recipient's social status, so that Cecilia prudently has a pew-opener's children 'coarsely brought up, having no intention to provide for them but by helping them to common employments'. Sentimental heroes, on the other hand, may pour out huge sums of money, but a wholesale change in society is not envisaged by any novelist until such revolutionary works of the 1790s as Holcroft's *Anna St Ives* (1792) or Godwin's *Caleb Williams* (1794).

Sentiment avoids any criticism of the economic structure of society. In *The Fool of Quality* Brooke closely associates the so-called 'eternal LAW OF BENEVOLENCE' with competitive capitalism (II, p32)—indeed, it depends upon the accumulation of private wealth for its operation—and his hero, Harry, observing 'the money amassed by the wealthy, to have been already extracted from the earnings of the poor', concludes that the objects of charity should be even more unfortunate than 'those from whom the money was exacted' (II, pp170-1), an argument which conveniently neglects the benefit the wealthy derive from the transaction. Sentimental tears are often a disclaimer of social guilt, and sentimental writing arises at least in part from the inadequacy of socially current ideas to understand and tackle the origins of social distress. Enemies of sentiment, like Maria Edgeworth, accurately reckoned it a 'luxury' of the well-to-do.

FANNY BURNEY

Fanny Burney was foremost among the novelists of this period who refused to grant sentiment pre-eminence over reason. Rejecting the sentimental morality of the 'heart', and the sentimental structure of reconciliation and redemption by 'change of heart', she sought to show the full worth of 'steadiness and prudence'. She put her trust in rational communication between people, despite its limitations, for she had no faith in the sympathetic action of 'a pulse in the soul'. Her emphasis was always on moral effort and right conduct, examined in a realistic fictional world. She thought the ending of her *Cecilia* (1782)

> somewhat original, for the hero and heroine are neither plunged in the depths of misery, nor exalted to UN*human* happiness. Is not such a middle state more natural, more according to real life, and less resembling every other book of fiction?

Her three important novels—*Evelina* (1778), *Cecilia* (1782) and *Camilla* (1796)—all concern 'the dangers run by Female Youth' when unprotected by 'the mother's careful wing' (*Camilla*, VIII.vi, OEN, pp645–6). The heroine is beset on all sides by mercenary suitors, the insults of the vulgar, and the bad example of fashionable extravagance. Camilla's subtlest hazard is the unregulated sensibility of the beautiful young Mrs Berlinton, who offers her sentimental friendship and excitement, but who gambles and dallies with men. These novels all centre on a doctrine of feminine prudence, embodied in *Camilla*, in Mr Tyrold's frequently reprinted advice to his daughter on 'the difficulties and the conduct of the female heart' (V.v, OEN, pp 353 and 355–62).

Burney is a deliberate moral teacher, holding up characters as warnings against such ruling passions as pride and greed, and also exposing a host of minor satirical characters to ridicule. But her novels too often have the flavour of conduct-books. Indeed she was not sure that the lax associations of the word 'novel' made it appropriate to her work, although eventually the queen even permitted the princesses to read *Cecilia*, after it was recommended by a bishop. Sensibility and tears were not banished, of course, since in all literature of this period only really bad characters are unable to weep on appropriate occasions, but Burney's emphasis is on the appropriateness of the emotion. She describes the proper role of sensibility within a fictional world governed by Johnsonian social and moral standards, and Edmund Burke was bestowing the highest Augustan praise when he complimented her on 'the natural vein of humour, the tender pathetic, the comprehensive and noble moral, and the sagacious observation' in *Cecilia*.

Fanny Burney is the best of those late-eighteenth-century novelists who rejected sentiment and romance in favour of an Augustan moral structure and style. *Evelina* and *Cecilia* are still readable, and it would be unfair if she were only remembered as an influence on Jane Austen, much as she is surpassed by Austen in quality, and in terms of strangeness and sensation, by her sentimental and gothic contemporaries.

CHAPTER 5

Gothic, Romantic and Heroic

When Charlotte Lennox wrote *The Female Quixote* in 1751–2, she had to go back to the old-fashioned French romances of the previous century to provide the cause of her heroine's derangement. In 1797–8, on the other hand, Jane Austen found quite up-to-date literary extravagances to mislead Catherine Morland, her heroine in *Northanger Abbey*. Around 1750, major novelists largely aimed at realism and conventional morality, but by the late 1790s there were vast numbers of so-called gothic novels, which in the pursuit of sensation seemed to reject all criteria of 'truth' to everyday life.

GOTHIC FICTION

The first of these gothic novels—Horace Walpole's *The Castle of Otranto* (1764)—takes place in a fantastic version of the author's own house, Strawberry Hill, fictionally expanded from a decorated villa into an ancient Italian castle. From the first the gothic is associated with dream versions of reality and perceptions of the irrationality which might normally be suppressed in waking life. In Richardson, irrational phenomena appear from time to time, rather as in a carefully regulated waking existence, showing through the interstices of the rational surface of life. In the gothic novel the subconscious, the dream, the nightmare, become the source of the story-pattern, and of the setting and the character typology too. Walpole and his successors, like Ann Radcliffe and M. G. Lewis, developed a whole repertoire of symbols and devices which kept their art strangely in touch with the sub-conscious, with all its attendant anarchy and alarms.

The Castle of Otranto is haunted by the gigantic ghost of the founder of the house, who warns of its coming destruction be-cause it has been usurped by the wicked Manfred. A monstrous plumed helmet falls from the sky and crushes the usurper's son on his wedding day, and the action goes on to involve a threatened virgin, a cruel villain, supernatural portents, underground passages and so on—in fact, numbers of the prefabricated parts from which gothic novels were to be made right up into the 1820s. In his preface to the second edition of *Otranto* Walpole said that the book was an attempt to unite the 'imagination and improbability' of romance with 'nature', because in recent fiction 'the great resources of fancy [had] been dammed up, by strict adherence to common life'. He meant to effect a 'Shakespearian' contrast by juxtaposing the 'sublime' experiences of the principal characters with the comic naïvety of the domestic ancillaries, in order to set 'the former in a stronger light'. Indeed the effect of this and many later gothic novels depends on a whole series of contrasts, between the elevated and the bathetic, the sublime and the beautiful, terror and pleasure, darkness and light, destructive passion and reason, and malignancy and innocent purity—and the psycho-analytical importance of the symbolic forms in which these oppositions appear is obvious. *The Castle of Otranto* and its even more vivid successors show a release of subconscious energy unprecedented in English eighteenth-century literature. Even readers innocent of Freudian theory easily recognise such a pattern as a virtuous heroine trapped between the hard demands of domineering parents and the fearful threats of the villain, or the dream situation of wandering through a perplexing labyrinth in which one stumbles over awful revelations in the form of skeletons, bloody robes or instruments of torture.

Smollett is credited with the very first gothic scene in English fiction in his *Ferdinand Count Fathom* of 1753. Renaldo is paying a nocturnal visit to where his Serafina, alias Monimia, supposedly lies buried:

> The uncommon darkness of the night, the solemn silence, the lonely situation of the place, conspired with the occasion of his coming, and the dismal images of his fancy, to produce a real rapture of gloomy expectation, which the whole world would not have persuaded him to disappoint. The clock struck twelve, the owl screeched from the ruined battlement, the door was opened by the sexton, who, by the light of a glimmering taper, conducted the despairing lover to a dreary isle, and stamped upon the ground with his foot, saying, 'Here the young lady lies interred.'
>
> (chapter 62, OEN, p317)

This passage from Smollett itemises atmospheric effects which are common to hundreds of later gothic stories: Renaldo's 'rapture of gloomy expectation'—at once so fearful and so pleasurable—looks forward to the almost ritual pauses of anticipation by which both characters and readers are wound up to the necessary pitch of 'enthusiastic' dread in many other novels, with an almost incantatory recitation of these established formulae.

Otranto is a supernatural novel written in an age of scepticism, and relies on the social survival of feelings associated with superstitions which the author and his public had in fact rationally rejected. In the 1790s Ann Radcliffe took this contradiction between credence and scepticism to a logical solution by purveying all the thrills and terrors of the haunted castle, and then providing a rational explanation of them at the end of the novel. This allowed her a greater certainty of tone. She had no need to be facetious about her own fictional material, and her effects of terror were correspondingly heightened. None the less she set her novels in a highly fanciful world. In contrast with her own enlightened late-eighteenth-century England it is a place of darkness and superstition, possessing all the worst cruelties that a Protestant imagination could attribute to fanatical Catholicism. The sixteenth-century France and Italy of *The Mysteries of Udolpho* (1794) and the mid-eighteenth-century Italy of *The Italian* (1797) are historically monstrous, but by submitting the rationality, education and taste of her enlightened characters to the will of her agents of terror—the feudal despots, the sadistic priests, monks and nuns, and the Inquisition—she dramatises the struggle by which, in the rationalist scheme of things, 'certainty' was achieved, at the personal and historical levels, against the anarchic forces of unreason.

Whether deliberately or not, Ann Radcliffe designed her novels in accord with the aesthetics of Edmund Burke's *Philosophical Enquiry into the Origin of our Ideas of the Sublime and the Beautiful*. Scenes of danger, fear, imprisonment or torture take place in sublime settings such as mountains with rocky crags and deep gorges, or dark, underground places, calculated in Burkean terms to inspire the emotion of terror, while normal social life is led amongst the smooth beauty of villas, gardens and vineyards. As Burke advocates, each condition is heightened by a contrast with its opposite—darkness with the light from a candle or a distant grating, the grandeur of mountain scenery with the faraway prospect of a fertile valley, or a pleasant garden outside Naples with the view of Vesuvius in the background. In the following passage from *The Italian* Ellena Rosalba exhibits the effects of a sublime landscape, together with the psychological heightening of her plight by the contrast of a pleasant memory, and finally the hard-won control of the self which her author favours. She has been abducted and soliloquises while being carried up into the mountains:

'If I am condemned to misery, surely I could endure it with more fortitude in scenes like these, than amidst the tamer landscapes of naturel Here, the objects seem to impart somewhat of their own force, their own sublimity, to the soul. . . .' But soon after the idea of Vivaldi [her lover] glancing athwart her memory, she melted into tears; the weakness however was momentary, and during the rest of the journey she preserved a strenuous equality of mind.

(I.vi, OEN, pp62–3)

Peace finally comes—as in *The Mysteries of Udolpho*—when the heroine and her suitor

> were, at length, restored to each other—to the felicity of this life,
> that of aspiring to moral and labouring for intellectual improve-
> ment—to the pleasures of enlightened society, and to the exercise
> of the benevolence, which had always animated their hearts . . .
>
> (IV.xix, OEN, p672)

The book ends with a high-toned affirmation of social order, property and inheritance, against the malignant and disorderly forces dramatised so vividly before. Yet the concluding platitude about the inevitable triumph of virtue over vice is only a conventional gesture. On the contrary, Radcliffe's fiction leaves the impression of a world where nameless fears lie in wait for even the staunchest upholders of morality and mental self-control.

In Radcliffe's scheme of things landscape is no arbitrary symbol for modes of life. For her, as for Burke, the taste requisite for its appreciation depends as much as moral conduct on a balance between judgement and sensibility, which can only be achieved by innate disposition plus education. At a time when landowners commonly commissioned landscape paintings to celebrate their possessions, Mrs Radcliffe gives one of her virtuous characters in *Udolpho* an authorial pat-on-the-back for surveying an extensive scene 'with the pride of conscious property, as well as the eye of taste' (III.xi, OEN, p481). The return to the plains is a return to bourgeois property as well as bourgeois morality.

Horrors of many sorts lurk behind the rational surface of life in Ann Radcliffe's world. In the work of the other most influential gothic novelist, Matthew Gregory Lewis, author of *The Monk* (1796), the psychological possibilities of Ann Radcliffe's gothic become physical actuality, and the dominant mode is no longer terror at potential horrors but revulsion at their realisation. In *The Monk*, nightmare takes over completely, instead of announcing itself fitfully as in Radcliffe when ordered social life is disrupted. Where the heroine of *The Mysteries of Udolpho* was frightened by the effigy of a corpse, Lewis's Agnes de Medina is forced into direct contact with rotting flesh when imprisoned in the vault of a convent where, she recounts,

> my hand rested upon something soft: I grasped it, and advanced it towards the light. Almighty God! . . . In spite of its putridity, and the worms which preyed upon it, I perceived a corrupted human head, and recognised the features of a Nun who had died some months before!
>
> (III.iv, OEN, p403)

In *The Italian*, in a covertly sexual scene, Ellena is nearly violated by the dagger of her putative father; in *The Monk* Antonia is actually raped by her brother in a charnel-house. In the world of *The Italian*, which can more or less be rationalised, the villain meets with a mundane fate, while in *The Monk* Ambrosio is carried away by the Devil and dropped, shattered in a valley, where he slowly dies:

> Myriads of insects . . . fastened upon his sores, darted their stings into his body . . . and inflicted on him tortures the most exquisite and insupportable. The Eagles of the rock tore his flesh piecemeal, and dug out his eye-balls with their crooked beaks. . . . Blind, maimed, helpless, and despairing, venting his rage in blasphemy and curses . . . six miserable days did the Villain languish.
>
> (III.v, OEN, p442)

Malignant and irrational passions drive Mrs Radcliffe's villains, but Lewis's evil characters are possessed by demons. The whole of *The Monk* has a dream atmosphere and dream structure, and rational explanation of its events is impossible. This frank capitulation to the supernatural was at the time attributed to the influence of German stories which Lewis (himself an important populariser of German literature in Britain) knew in the original. Supernatural thrills obviously offended conservative literary taste, and more than one Tory defender of the old Augustan standards would have boasted that

No German nonsense sways my English heart,
Unus'd at ghosts and rattling bones to start.

But meanwhile, in Byron's phrase, 'tales of terror jostle[d] on the road', and strange story-patterns and evocative figures, such as the enigmatic Wandering Jew, were also imported into English literature from the German.

'Monk' Lewis's most striking addition to the gothic strain of fiction, apart from his blatant irreligion, was his open though often deviant eroticism. A fictional probing of the subconscious could now go much further, and profit succeeding writers for a century to come. The scene in which Don Raymond goes to embrace his mistress in the dark, only to find the galvanised corpse of the 'Bleeding Nun' in his arms, expresses a deep unease with sexuality; and when the beautiful Matilda, the model for Ambrosio's image of the Madonna, suddenly displays a demonic sexual appetite in bed, Lewis exposes a male fear which can be traced in this form at least as far as Huysmans's *Là-bas* (1891). The dream-basis of *The Monk* is made clear in a nightmare Lorenzo has of his bride, Antonia, being snatched from him at the altar by a monster which plunges with her into a flaming gulf, as the cathedral crumbles around them, and she escapes upwards, leaving only her pure white robe in the fiend's possession (I.i, OEN, pp27–8). This nightmare prefigures the story-pattern of the novel as a whole, demonstrating how gothic fiction, like the dreaming mind, dismembers the psyche, and personifies its different aspects, setting them in dramatic conflict with each other. So this least 'true to life' of English fiction has more immediate access to the subconscious than many great realistic masterpieces of the literature.

To present this extraordinary fictional material, Lewis and his compeers had largely to reject the advances in realistic narration and dialogue made by novelists like Richardson, having recourse instead to summary modes of narration close to those in use a century earlier, before the flowering of the fiction of everyday life. The additional stylistic resource which Lewis brought to his narrative was something of the elegance and wit of his political patron William Beckford, whose oriental extravaganza *Vathek* had managed to unite an even more ambitious amalgam of the sensuality and magic of the Arabian Nights with the author's own odd humour and particular amorous propensities. *Vathek*, originally written in French and first published in an English translation by Samuel Henley in 1786, was none the less a strong influence for accuracy in literary orientalism. Beckford actually read Arabic, and helped to invalidate Goldsmith's taunt about earlier orientalism, that 'every advance made towards sense, is only a deviation from sound. Eastern tales should always be sonorous, lofty, musical and unmeaning'. Beckford replaced sonority with urbanity, and senselessness with outlandish but powerful psychological images, and the stylistic skill with which he achieved this is his most direct link with the gothic of Lewis. An important ingredient in the literary compound of *The Monk* was ballad-poetry, which Coleridge praised in a letter to Wordsworth in 1798, for its 'rare merit' of natural, modern language and simplicity. Yet it was as a novelist and dramatist that Lewis had his lasting influence. He was a great adapter of German drama for the British stage, while his own *Monk* and 'The Ballad of Alonzo the Brave and Fair Imogene' which it contained were presented in every dramatic form available at the time, from melodrama to ballet. It is well known that melodrama fed Victorian novelists, like Dickens; its own earlier debt to prose fiction should not be forgotten.

The line of gothic fiction in English continues into the first decades of the nineteenth century, when the masterpiece of suggestive terror, repulsive horror and constructive ingenuity is undoubtedly *Melmoth the Wanderer* (1820), by Scott's protégé Charles Maturin. Melmoth has bought himself a tormenting immortality from the Devil, on the condition that he can escape it if, but only if, he finds another man willing to exchange his lot with him. The Wanderer lives through centuries, reappearing eerily in numbers of contrasting stories which are set within each other like Chinese boxes, violently juxtaposing moods as different as primeval innocence and the gothic horrors of the Inquisition. At times Maturin gives alarmingly free rein to some of the blackest views of human nature to be found in the whole of English literature.

Ever since the heyday of the gothic novel its techniques have been used for scenes of sensation or for atmosphere, by writers as various as Edgar Allan Poe, Victor Hugo, Charles Dickens, Emily Brontë, Wilkie Collins and Bram Stoker (not to mention Hammer Films today). In the adaptation of old strategies of terror and mystery to new ends, the mystery is often transferred from the gothic castle to the great city. The labyrinth and its attendant dangers are no longer buried beneath convents and medieval ruins, but hidden in the warrens and rookeries of London and Paris, and even the complex web of 'respectable' urban life. The labyrinth in *Oliver Twist* or *Martin Chuzzlewit*, or some of Poe's *Tales of Mystery*, or Wilkie Collins's *Woman in White* and many subsequent detective stories, are all in part a response to the huge complexity of the modern city, where people live together by the million. Often, like Dickens's early persona 'Boz', the writer claims a privileged understanding of the metropolis, but it is really beyond human comprehension. Inevitably a new image of the city emerges by the end of the century. It is now the totally alienated hell of James Thomson's great poem, *The City of Dreadful Night* (1874), or of T. S. Eliot's *Waste Land* (1923)—a disintegrated world in which only the blind seer Tiresias has seen and understood all. Even if only a minority of the myriad gothic novels which had their hour in the decades around 1800 are still worth reading today, gothic fiction has a special place in the development of the modern urban imagination.

Meanwhile writers in various languages exploited just the kind of German material which 'Monk' Lewis used in the 1790s, such as the nineteenth century's favourite demonic effect of the Doppelgänger—a person's ghostly double which haunts him throughout his life. Obvious examples are Mary Shelley in her *Frankenstein* (1818), Hans Christian Andersen in 'The Shadow' ('Skygget', 1847), Dickens in his Christmas Book *The Haunted Man* (1848), or Robert Louis Stevenson in *Dr Jekyll and Mr Hyde* (1886); and, most interesting of all, *The Private Memoirs and Confessions of a Justified Sinner* (1824) by James Hogg, who stiffened the supernatural with theology in a peculiarly Scottish examination of an extreme Calvinist mentality, by which he attacked the doctrine of 'effectual calling'. The protagonist of this 'strange tale of Diablerie and Theology' holds the antinomian belief that he is allowed to transgress all moral laws because he is pre-elected to grace, and cannot lose his future place in heaven by any sin he may commit on earth, including matricide. The story of this 'justified sinner' is told twice: once through a third-person 'editor' who tries to see things 'objectively', and then by the subject himself, who believes in his spiritual pride that he has been doing God's work in ridding the world of non-elect persons, and laying 'the strong holds on sin and Satan as flat . . . as the dung that is spread out to fatten the land' (OEN, p13). For all the novel's insight into theology and psychopathology, and its narrative ingenuity, it turned out not to be a useful model for subsequent British fiction—unless, as is likely, Emily Brontë was stimulated by it in writing *Wuthering Heights* (1847). Yet *The Memoirs and Confessions* now reads as the most 'modern' and compelling novel of its period.

The most immediate contribution of gothic fiction proper to any other branch of literature came about through the transformation of the gothic villain into a romantic hero-type often used by Byron. Manfred's 'severe temper', 'exquisite villainy', 'remorse' and frequent 'tempest of mind' in Walpole's *Castle of Otranto* (Everyman, pp111 and 127) established a type which Ann Radcliffe developed in Montoni, the villain of *The Mysteries of Udolpho*, with his fierce brooding, his nameless crimes and his unruly band of dependants whom only he could manage. Then, in *The Monk*, Lewis psychologised the villain. Ambrosio, so pious, so seemingly perfect, so eloquent in his preaching, has a great nature which has been deformed by his upbringing, so that he is tormented by the opposite tugs of severe self-discipline and monumental vice:

> He was naturally enterprizing, firm, and fearless ... There was no want of generosity in his nature ... His abilities were quick and shining, and his judgment vast, solid, and decisive. ... His Instructors carefully repressed those virtues, whose grandeur and disinterestedness were ill-suited to the Cloister. ... He was suffered to be proud, vain, ambitious, and disdainful ... He was implacable when offended, and cruel in his revenge. Still in spite of the pains taken to pervert them, his natural good qualities would occasionally break through ...
>
> (II.iii, OEN, pp236–7)

The moral ambivalence of such a character is the pivot between straightforward villainy and romantic heroism. Ambrosio has guilty sex with a demonic woman, then murders at the prompting of his lechery, rapes his dying sister between two rotting corpses, and finally sells his soul to the devil.

From now on the gothic villain is the battleground of the super-ego and the id. Encouraged by Lewis's example, Ann Radcliffe created in Schedoni, the monk who masterminds the evil in *The Italian*, a tormented, solitary, passionate and strangely powerful individual, whose physiognomy

> bore traces of many passions, which seemed to have fixed the features they no longer animated. An habitual gloom and severity prevailed over the deep lines of his countenance; and his eyes were so piercing that they seemed to penetrate ... into the hearts of men, and to read their most secret thoughts ...
>
> (I.ii, OEN, p35)

ROMANTIC HEROISM

For the heroes of his dramas and most of his verse tales, except for *Beppo* and *Don Juan*, Byron creates a similar passionate and powerful type. He obviously draws on Schedoni for his description of Hassan, the guilt-ridden hero of *The Giaour* (1813), who has taken refuge in a monastery:

> Dark and unearthly is the scowl
> That glares beneath his dusky cowl.
> *(The Giaour*, 832–3)

He has

> A spirit yet unquell'd and high,
> That claims and keeps ascendency;
> (840–1)

and, like Ambrosio and Schedoni, he possesses the potential for great virtue mingled with his vice, having features

> Which speak a mind not all degraded
> Even by the crimes through which it waded
> (864–5)

Close examination reveals many verbal parallels with gothic novels, while the Giaour's piercing eye is derived not only from Schedoni but, like the title of the poem and indeed much of Byron's oriental enthusiasm, from Beckford's *Vathek*.

Such characters are clearly heroic not from their perfections but from their stature. Moral ambivalence is at the core of the type, and mingled attraction and alarm the required public reaction, the *Edinburgh Review*, for one, drawing attention to 'something *piquant* in the very novelty and singularity of that cast of misanthropy and universal scorn, which we have already noticed as among the repulsive features' of cantos 1 and 2 of *Childe Harold's Pilgrimage* (XIX, 467). Byron had had prose models other than Walpole, Radcliffe and Lewis, such as John Moore's *Zeluco* (1789) which was one of his favourite novels as a boy. This is a third-person narrative of the sort of career which would have made a picaresque novel, but Moore has shifted the interest from the declared moral 'that Vice leads to endless misery in a future state' to the psychological turbulence of the 'inward misery' which accompanies it in this life. Zeluco is a passionate villain, apparently predestined to evil, who ends by strangling his child in the belief that it is the incestuous offspring of his wife by her brother. As a contemporary reader in Glasgow College Library commented in the margin, 'What a monster this Zeluco is and yet he has some good qualities.' Samuel Johnson denounced characters in whom good and bad qualities were mixed as likely to undermine the reader's sense of moral discrimination, but Byron and his admirers—literary, social and sexual—saw things quite differently, and derived their excitement from just this moral paradox.

Like the hero of Shelley's 'Alastor' and many other romantic questers in European literature, Byron's Manfred seeks the secrets of existence in a search of charnel-houses like that which provides the 'modern Prometheus', Frankenstein, with the materials and knowledge necessary to create his monster. The Faustian sin of desiring knowledge at any cost drives a character like Manfred on to '[c]onclusions most forbidden' (II.ii, 83), forcing him at last to wander the mountain-tops in desolate guilt. This kind of romantic hero has strong affinities with Milton's Satan—interpreted in this new age of revolution as a hero in revolt against God's despotism—and echoes Satan's despairing cry

> Which way I flie is Hell; my self am Hell
> (*Paradise Lost*, IV, 75)

It is apt that Frankenstein's monster—that case of natural innocence perverted by total human estrangement—should practise reading on a copy of *Paradise Lost*, and feel mingled pleasure and demonic rage at the happiness of Adam and Eve before the fall.

The majority of Victorian novels of any stature had little room in them for a heroic-romantic streak, with the one important exception of Emily Brontë's *Wuthering Heights*. Love, the all-consuming, destroying passion, the romantic hero, wild, dangerous, uncouth and demonic—these stand in the Byronic tradition; and indeed Emily Brontë had already tried out many of Heathcliff's principal traits in verse which bears a distinct Byronic stamp. There are important developments in Emily Brontë's handling of romantic heroism. First, the woman becomes more important, and is psychologically investigated to a depth which few other Victorian writers were daring enough to emulate. Then violent passion is set against an ordered and 'respectable' modern life—the wildness of the heath against the restrictions of civilisation; Wuthering Heights against Thrushcross Grange—to display the limitations of mere duty, as Heathcliff detects them in Catherine's married life with Edgar Linton:

> You talk of her mind being unsettled—How the devil could it be otherwise, in her frightful isolation? And that insipid, paltry creature attending her from *duty* and *humanity*! From *pity* and *charity*! He might as well plant an oak in a flower-pot, and expect it to thrive, as imagine he can restore her to vigour in the soil of his shallow cares!
>
> (chapter 14, PEL, p190)

The author's identification with the heath, not the valleys, puts her outside the mainstream of Victorian middle-class cultural life, but is her great and enduring strength, making this novel the most energetic protest of all against the confinement of Early-Victorian society.

Other Victorian characters with more-or-less Byronic traits are seen from the opposite point of view—that is, as outsiders, threats or oddities—like the little professor, Paul Emmanuel, in Charlotte Brontë's *Villette* (1853):

> His passions were strong, his aversions and attachments alike vivid; the force he exerted in holding both in check by no means mitigated an observer's sense of their vehemence . . . he often excited in ordinary minds fear and dislike. . . .
>
> (chapter 19, Pan Classics, p196)

Paul Emmanuel is a Byronic or Napoleonic miniature. The full-blown Byronic hero is usually too unruly for Victorian fiction, and perhaps too rarely met with in respectable middle-class society to accord with many writers' notions of fidelity to every-day life.

Byronism, however, was international, and inextricably linked on the Continent with struggles for national independence and individualism against the legitimism of the Congress of Vienna. Charlotte Brontë was responding accurately to European streams of thought when she associated her small-scale Byronic professor with 'political convictions and national feelings' that indicated the Europe-wide movement of liberal, democratic nationalism (*Villette*, chapter 27, Pan Classics, p301).

In the high Victorian period, the expansive character transcending the smallness of everyday life could no longer be a gothic villain or Byronic hero. Instead the complex of emotions associated with these problematic characters becomes attached to the enterprising capitalist or industrialist—either the sort of man whom Carlyle celebrated in *Past and Present* (1843) as a Captain of Industry, or one of the 'Gamblers swollen *big*' whom he condemned in his *Latter-Day Pamphlets* in 1850. The moral ambivalence of Byronism now surrounds large-scale speculators—men necessary in a rapidly expanding economy, but frequently unethical if not outright criminal, even by accepted business standards. Mid-Victorian periodical criticism shows a cultural craving for grandeur in fictional characters, and an almost Byronic streak can be seen in some critics' responses to a character like Anthony Trollope's great swindler Melmotte in *The Way We Live Now* (1874–5), though in the novel itself, there is nothing grand about the man:

> His hero is a swindler, and by his audacity and the magnitude of his operations, rises almost into respectability out of the base level of meaner worthlessness . . . His is a life of fraud demanding such constant vigilance, such habits of self-control, such foresight and preparation, such self-reliance and courage, that it is almost great.

73

It is impossible not to sympathize in a degree with a struggle so manfully maintained . . .

(*Saturday Review*, 17 July 1875)

This critic's moral ambivalence can be paralleled by attitudes to real-life speculators and in particular to that daring stock-manipulator and account-cooker, George Hudson, 'the Railway King'. *The Times*, which had been most energetic in exposing him twenty years before, summed up the hero-villain syndrome in its obituary notice of 14 December 1871:

He was a man who united largeness of view with wonderful speculative courage. He went in for bigger things than any one else. . . . This is the kind of man who leads the world.

The grand speculator is fitly seen in the same terms as the Byronic hero, as one of the 'solitary . . . selected people', like Ibsen's swindler, John Gabriel Borkman, in his play of 1896, whose heroic cry of self-assertion and his identification with Napoleon fit the whole complex of Byronic and Faustian feelings. Borkman acted as he did 'because I was John Gabriel Borkman,—and not anyone else'. Like the romantic hero, he was predestined to greatness and sin by '[c]ompulsive necessity', and his sin of killing love and his resulting isolation fit the pattern of works like Byron's *Manfred*. But, as used by Ibsen, they now reveal the contradictions inherent in nineteenth-century economic individualism. This is what makes Ibsen the supreme diagnostician of the moral corruption of Victorian high-capitalism, not in Scandinavia alone, but throughout industrialised Europe.

Ibsen's dishonest financier is a world away from the gothic villain of a hundred years before, but he shares with the literary descendants of Ambrosio and Schedoni the problematic moral values with which various writers exposed and challenged social orthodoxy. The Marquis de Sade, a great admirer of 'Monk' Lewis (as well as of Richardson, incidentally), proposed that gothic fiction arose in response to the real-life horrors of the last decade of the eighteenth century; and, while the spate of translations of English gothic novels into French in 1796 proves them to have found ready readers in that violent year, de Sade's explanation will not do, if only because the genre was established before the French Revolution, and in Britain, a country at a very different stage of political development. Yet the deliberate attack on Augustan literary conventions and restraints must, as much as political revolution, be seen as part of the general destruction of earlier eighteenth-century optimism.

LATE-EIGHTEENTH-CENTURY ROMANCE

In this respect gothic fiction was one of a number of signs of cultural change, including sentiment, too, and a vogue for a new kind of romance late in the century. Such types of fiction stand in contrast to Clara Reeve's famous definition of the novel, as she understood the word in 1785:

> The Novel gives a familiar relation of such things, as pass every day before our eyes, such as may happen to our friend, or to ourselves; and the perfection of it, is to represent every scene, in so easy and natural a manner, and to make them appear so probable, as to deceive us into a persuasion (at least while we are reading) that all is real, until we are affected by the joys or distresses, of the persons in the story, as if they were our own.

In this sense it was 'novels' that Fanny Burney wrote and, after her, Jane Austen and a stream of Victorians, among whom Anthony Trollope, for one, closely follows Reeve in stating that a novel should give 'a picture of common life enlivened by humour and sweetened by pathos'. Through Reeve one can see a link between Samuel Johnson's critical standards and one of the dominant modes of Victorian fiction.

The form of less 'natural' fiction that constituted late-eighteenth-century romance was mercilessly parodied by Jane Austen in her youth, in *Love and Freindship*:

My Father was a native of Ireland and an inhabitant of Wales; my Mother was the natural Daughter of a Scotch Peer by an italian Opera-girl—I was born in Spain and received my Education at a Convent in France. . . .

In my Mind, every Virtue that could adorn it was centered; it was the Rendez-vous of every good Quality and of every noble sentiment.

A sensibility too tremblingly alive to every affliction of my Freinds, my Acquaintance and particularly to every affliction of my own, was my only fault, if a fault it could be called. Alas! how altered now! . . . My accomplishments too, begin to fade . . . and I have entirely forgot the *Minuet Dela Cour*.

Once again it was German literature that was accused of inciting the extravagances Austen was parodying. In *Emmeline, Orphan of the Castle* (1788) Charlotte Smith was adopting a carefully moderate position in having her heroine enjoy both Goethe's *The Sorrows of Werter* and Fanny Burney's *Cecilia*.

POLITICAL NOVELS

The novels so far discussed were not directly political, but in the 1790s Thomas Holcroft and William Godwin both deliberately used novels as vehicles for their political beliefs. Holcroft openly challenged the existing social and economic system, by propagating the perfectibilist ideals of the early phases of the French Revolution. (He was indicted for high treason in 1794.) In *Anna St Ives* (1792) he marries his heroine, a baronet's daughter, to the son of her father's gardener, to prove the need to restructure society by valuing people according to their personal worth rather than their birth and wealth. As an advanced feminist, Holcroft wished a woman to be an educated, independently-minded person, in all ways mentally and morally the equal of men. Anna St Ives goes so far as to doubt the need for marriage in an ideal society, and meets a standard anti-feminist response from a rake who illogically demands that she should follow her principles by becoming his mistress. She declines, he abducts her, but—where Richardson's Harriet Byron needed Sir Charles Grandison to rescue her—Anna St Ives beats off her would-be rapist by the force of her own personality. Holcroft's was a bold fictional affront to orthodox social thinking. It was not for nothing that he was the friend of William Godwin, author of *Political Justice*, and of Mary Wollstonecraft, author of *A Vindication of the Rights of Woman*.

Godwin's own novel *Caleb Williams* (1794) was another violent attack on standard eighteenth-century optimism. All was certainly not for the best in the best possible world in this book. Far from presenting a picture of squire and tenantry linked by benevolent paternalism, Godwin pointed to the blatant exploitation of the lower classes by the ruling class who had exclusive possession of justice in the countryside, where the landlord was also the magistrate. In contrast to Holcroft's coolly cerebral writing, Godwin produced one of the most vivid and concentrated psychological studies of the age in this first-person narrative of persecution and almost demonic obsession. Only Hogg's *Justified Sinner* surpasses him in this respect. Holcroft and Godwin were a major influence on Shelley and on nineteenth-century British socialism, yet their novels are less read today than they deserve.

COMIC SATIRE

The ideas which occupied intelligent minds in the 1790s and early 1800s are all hilariously aired in the novels of the greatest prose satirist of the age, Thomas Love Peacock. He began his career with rather luke-warm sentimental poetry, but became committed to satire after a visit to Shelley at Bracknell in 1813, where he was brought up against a strange set of enthusiasts who, as he later explained, directly provoked his conversational novels in the following years, and *Headlong Hall* (1815) in particular:

Every one of them adopting some of the articles of the faith of their general church, had each nevertheless some predominant crochet of his or her own, which left a number of open questions for earnest and not always temperate discussion. I was sometimes irreverent enough to laugh at the fervour with which opinions utterly unconducive to any practical result were battled for as matters of the highest importance to the well-being of mankind . . .

The criticism of the ideas as 'unconducive to any practical result' does not put Peacock into the Benthamite camp, for he was equally quick to expose the weaknesses of the Utilitarian position, and his reaction to the Mills when he came to know them was very like his reaction to the Bracknell set.

He loved to find weaknesses in what he considered extreme or untenable positions, even when the object of the satire was a close friend and the position one with which he himself felt a considerable sympathy. The result is that his characters are often coherent spokesmen of the positions they represent. Mr Cypress's Byronic song in *Nightmare Abbey* (1818), for instance, is such a sympathetic parody that it is a good example of the style it supposedly mocks, while we know that Peacock planned a poem in celebration of J. F. Newton's system of astrology, at the same time as he was satirising just this kind of notion in prose. This is good-natured, not cynical, satire and Peacock's tolerant view of comedy is seen in all its humanity in *Maid Marian* (1822), when Friar John says, 'The worst thing is good enough to be laughed at, though it be good for nothing else; and the best thing, though it be good for something else, is good for nothing better.'

Peacock does not satirise from any consistent philosophical and political viewpoint. Strong, often philistine commonsense is the only constant, and his satire is based on the perception of the incompatibility of anything, past, present or future, with this standard. His criticism of his character's crochets acts rather like the dawn in the first sentence of *Headlong Hall*: 'The ambiguous light of a December morning, peeping through the windows of the Holyhead mail, dispelled the soft visions of the four insides . . .'

His attitude towards any given issue is ambivalent. He is an emotional conservative, in touch with the most advanced thought of his age.

The Victorians regarded Peacock as a mere eccentric, and his books had little lasting influence, because they could scarcely be encompassed by the term 'novel' as generally understood later in the nineteenth century. They are comic masterpieces, but of a rare sort. Victorian fiction was to take many of its major characteristics from Peacock's great contemporaries: Jane Austen and Sir Walter Scott.

CHAPTER 6

Austen, Scott and the Victorians

Two contemporaries could scarcely be less alike than Jane Austen and Sir Walter Scott, she restricting her fiction to the most common events of everyday life among a few well-to-do families in the south of England, and he taking adventure and the great events of history for his theme. Writing of Austen, Scott said

> The Big Bow wow strain I can do myself like any now going but the exquisite touch which renders ordinary common-place things and characters interesting from the truth of the description and the sentiment is denied to me.

Nothing could aspire less to the 'Big Bow wow strain' than Austen's carefully limited and reined-in art. The two authors were as great a contrast in their lives and reputations. Austen was personally unknown in her lifetime, and undervalued for decades afterwards by all but a handful of admirers, while Scott was fêted in his day, lamented after his death, and remained the enthusiasm of all Europe for much of the century. Yet between them, in their different ways, these two developed the techniques which were to be used by the Victorian realists, and provide future genera-tions of novelists with the means of embodying their vision of human life and society.

JANE AUSTEN

Austen's *forte* was to reveal the ethical basis of everyday life, and show how the ordinary occurrences of the world, no less than great actions, were centred on moral convention, moral judgement and moral choice, so that living in society required a constant alertness of will and intellect to control the self and understand others. With this view of life, it would be impossible to present characters as autonomous essences, independent of the world around them, although Austen frequently describes a person and then proceeds to show him or her performing actions which correspond to the personality—in this sense character precedes action in her work and is not formed by it. But, for her, character is so much a result of education and upbringing, environment, and financial and social status all acting on innate disposition, that in her hands a study of any small group of people inevitably carries with it the analysis of the outlook, way-of-life and *mores* of a whole segment of society.

Oppositions between contrasting life-styles are structurally central to her novels, but the subtlety of the analysis forbids a simple equation of outlook with social status as much as with inborn characteristics. Personality is a complex product of both, while the public persona which interacts with others in daily life has an additional overlay of social attributes, such as wealth and rank. Human existence is necessarily social and the novelist must build on interpersonal perceptions as well as individual case-studies. Because Austen is supremely successful in demonstrating the psychological and social mechanisms of life, her novels are still among the best reading for those who wish to understand the full richness of everyday human relations, even though things like elopement, divorce or disrespect for the Established Church do not in themselves strike us as forcibly as they did Austen's society.

The deliberate bounds she imposed on her fictional action and her language in no way represent a narrowing of the possibilities of the novel. If so much can be adduced from such small gestures, it is reasonable to prefer her restrained approach, with its high power-to-weight ratio, to art which depends upon sheer size to impress the beholder. Nevertheless Austen suffered for a long time under an outmoded hierarchy of literary kinds in which she was rated below works which could claim an epic or a tragic importance. In fact, the narrow scope of her fiction is essential to its impact, because hers is a type of art in which the pressure, as it were, is increased by confinement, so that the slightest straining at the bounds is enormously significant. Full critical appreciation of her work is only possible to those with a fine sensitivity to narrative language and the minutiae of characters' linguistic and other behaviour.

Her concentration on the moral significance of life in well-to-do circles—what Edmund, in *Mansfield Park* (OEN, p193), calls 'the middle state of worldly circumstances'—imposes fruitful bounds to begin with. Although hers is a very different world from Defoe's—the squirearchy is her emotional centre, not the economic adventurer—the choice of some version of 'the middle state' always seems to have stimulated the best English novelists. The two-sided social opposition from above and below produces a concentrated attention on different aspects of middle-class values from Defoe's time to the present, such as it would be hard to parallel for persistence and subtlety in any other analysis of class ideology.

The subject of middle-class behaviour, as Jane Austen inherits it, derives from Fanny Burney and, behind her, Samuel Richardson—both of whom sought to defend the morality of their class against the twin threats of contaminating vulgarity from below and the false allure of the aristocratic life above. As they were dealing with the most socially mobile groups in their societies, their standards required constant definition and redefinition, largely by means of scenes of interaction across status lines, such as became the basic material of English society fiction for a couple of centuries. Austen improved on her predecessors. Where

Richardson was complacent in celebrating the values his social position relied upon, she is secure enough to allow herself to be more knowingly ambivalent, presenting her picture through a complex refracting medium of ironic narrative, which prevents a facile verdict on just where the author stands and hence leaves important attitudes in a state of fruitful tension. She is more subtle than Burney, who presented her social threats in the form of characters which, although vivid and effective, were too much in the 'humours' tradition not to jar against the realistically developed central characters with whom all her sympathy lay. One of Austen's developments is to use similar modes of presentation for all her characters, so that closely similar styles of language can be applied to the speech, thought and associated narrative of them all; and, although there is a loss of lower-middle-class characters, there is a gain in avoiding a system of characterisation which had to treat them condescendingly.

There is a very developed sense in Austen that words are social property, not only defined in terms of the history of the language but embodying a whole complex of community attitudes too, and coloured in addition by the specialised usage of particular groups or types of people. Almost any sentence from her six novels would illustrate this. When in *Sense and Sensibility* (1811) Mrs Dashwood and her daughters move home, for example, the narrative sets the domestic convenience implied in the word 'house' up against a false but picturesque idea of 'cottage':

> As a house, Barton Cottage, though small, was comfortable and compact; but as a cottage it was defective, for the building was regular, the roof was tiled, the window shutters were not painted green, nor were the walls covered with honeysuckles.
>
> (I.vi, OEN, p23)

The opinions of the Miss Bertrams on Mary Crawford's brother in *Mansfield Park* (1814) are expressed in terms appropriate to them as, in their own eyes, 'the finest young women in the country':

> Her brother was not handsome; no, when they first saw him, he
> was absolutely plain, black and plain . . . The second meeting
> proved him not so very plain . . . and after a third interview
> . . . he was no longer allowed to be called so by any body. He was,
> in fact, the most agreeable young man the sisters had ever
> known . . .
>
> (I.v, OEN, p39)

This is the language of narrative summary, heavily coloured by
the characteristic usages and habits of thought of those in the
Miss Bertrams' position.

In a similar way, the narrative language can draw attention to
larger contrasts, like that between the decorum of Mansfield Park
and the dangerous follies of 'fast' life:

> The Honourable John Yates, this new friend, had not much to
> recommend him beyond habits of fashion and expense, and being
> the younger son of a lord with a tolerable independence; and Sir
> Thomas would probably have thought his introduction at Mans-
> field by no means desirable.
>
> (I.xiii, OEN, p109)

Tom Bertram's view is glanced at in 'friend', and the standards of
the extravagant set he and Yates move in are discredited by the
device of treating them rhetorically for the nonce as though they
were the virtues these young men construe them as, so that the 'by
no means desirable' concludes the sentence with all the force
which ironic understatement can lend.

These three examples show Jane Austen aiming at modish follies
and vanities, but elsewhere she uses similar techniques to question
her society in larger terms, by indicating views supposedly held
quite validly by the world at large, and which the authorial voice
pretends to take seriously, before proceeding to undermine them,
until the communal opinion is seen as nonsense, and not the
receptacle of 'common sense' that the reader was invited to consider it. The most discussed sentence in all English fiction, the

opening of *Pride and Prejudice*, is a brief example: 'It is a truth universally acknowledged, that a single man in possession of a good fortune, must be in want of a wife.' First of all, the 'truth' is shown to be the wishful thinking of his neighbours, and the universe by which it is held merely 'the surrounding families'. By the time the opinion has been elaborated by Mrs Bennett it has become silly and, by the end of a very short chapter, its mouth-piece has been summed up as 'a woman of mean understanding, little information, and uncertain temper' (I.i, OEN, p3).

In the face of myriad examples like this, it is impossible to believe in a limited, complacent Jane Austen, quite at home in the narrow world she inhabited. Her voice is so much more intelligent than the society whose values she at first seems to celebrate. Her favourite rhetorical strategy is to present social or family dogma quite quietly as though innocent of harm; then to push an ironic wedge between it and her own authorial standpoint, and end in open sarcasm:

> The Miss Bertrams were now fully established among the belles of the neighbourhood; and as they joined to beauty and brilliant acquirements, a manner naturally easy, and carefully formed to general civility and obligingness, they possessed its favour as well as its admiration. Their vanity was in such good order, that they seemed to be quite free from it, and gave themselves no airs; while the praises attending such behaviour ... served to strengthen them in believing they had no faults.
>
> (*Mansfield Park*, I.iv, OEN, p30)

The deficiency of social judgements of self and others, and the interdependence of a sense of self and public opinion have never been more economically displayed. Here, as often, Austen works by nuances of language which involve the feigned short-term acceptance by the authorial voice of the opinions and standards under attack.

This ever-shifting ironic attitude in the narrative gives the impression that Austen is simultaneously defining and question-ing orthodox moral standards, enabling her to build on an apparently stable, commonplace morality after a Johnsonian model, a fiction which in fact investigates its limitations and exposes the contradictions inherent in commonsense notions about existence. On one hand the heroine of *Mansfield Park*, Fanny Price, is established as a paragon, in contrast to the vanities and loosenesses of her Bertram cousins and Mary Crawford, and yet she is treated with touches of authorial irony which suggest—though they do not spell out—severe limitations. Virtue is made less than wholly attractive, not—as in Burney, say—merely because the paragons turn out to be boring, but with Austen's authorial awareness. What would have been more in the nature of plain assertion and exemplification of 'correct' principles in Richardson or Burney becomes in Austen a delicately managed tension between acceptance and rejection of social norms.

Austen's greatest contribution to the art of fiction was thoroughly to exploit existing techniques of fictional speech and narrative in order to achieve her subtle analyses of character and society as economically as possible, and to convey to the reader in a few lines what most eighteenth-century novelists would have developed into an extended aria or lengthy description. (Mrs Siddons could hardly have felt of any Austen character as she did of Burney's Cecilia, that '[t]here was no part she had ever so much wished to act'.) Austen was, in fact, the greatest practitioner of the novel of ordinary life in an age when authors were increasingly able to create one variegated surface out of narrative report, direct speech, reported speech and free indirect speech. A typical example occurs when Emma has severely misjudged Mr Elton's feelings and cruelly encouraged Harriet to expect an impossible proposal from him:

> Emma and Harriet had been walking together one morning, and, in Emma's opinion, been talking enough of Mr. Elton for that day. She could not think that Harriet's solace or her own sins required more; and she was therefore industriously getting rid of the subject as they returned;—but it burst out again when she thought she had succeeded, and after speaking some time of what the poor

must suffer in winter, and receiving no other answer than a very plaintive—'Mr. Elton is so good to the poor!' she found something else must be done.

(Emma, II.i, OEN, p137)

For rapid effects and subtle shifts of emphasis, Austen's narrative language half-assumes the modes of thought and expression of her characters, so that their consciousnesses are seen filtered through the central authorial intelligence, and more can be understood briefly from the authorial tone-of-voice than from straightforward report or direct speech.

Austen has all current styles at her command and, in the following example of Smollettian flow, conveys in less than half a page a monologue from Mrs Elton which lasts for 'half an hour' while she is picking strawberries:

—Delightful to gather for one's self—the only way of really enjoying them.—Morning decidedly the best time—never tired—every sort good—hautboy infinitely superior—no comparison—the others hardly eatable— . . . price of strawberries in London—abundance about Bristol— . . . cultivation—beds when to be renewed—gardeners thinking exactly different—no general rule—. . . delicious fruit—only too rich to be eaten much of—inferior to cherries— . . . only objection to gathering strawberries the stooping—glaring sun—tired to death—could bear it no longer—must go and sit in the shade.

(Emma, III.vi, OEN, p324)

This is not just represented speech, as it would usually be in Smollett, but action too, and amazingly economical.

Austen exploited all the means available at the time for representing thought as well as speech. In cases like that when the heroine of *Persuasion* is in turmoil because she cannot reveal the state of her affections to Captain Wentworth, a character's thoughts are rapidly incorporated, like 'submerged speech', hardly disturbing the narrative fluency:

Jealousy of Mr. Elliott! . . . Captain Wentworth jealous of her

affection! Could she have believed it a week ago—three hours ago!
For a moment the gratification was exquisite. But alas! there were
very different thoughts to succeed. How was such jealousy to be
quieted? How was the truth to reach him? How, in all the peculiar
disadvantages of their respective situations, would he ever learn
her real sentiments?

(II.viii, OEN, p398)

Techniques like this allow a growth of inwardness in character,
without the often awkward need for dramatic expression. Incidentally this passage identifies a major plot device which Austen
inherits from Richardson and Burney, and which generates a
story by imposing conventional obstacles to communication between the lovers, so that the heroine is left as the register of feelings without offending the *convenances* by being active in her love
affair.

Such semi-dramatic thought summaries—what Trollope was to
call 'unspoken soliloquies'—are found in embryo in Burney, and
the following example from *Cecilia* shows how the varying of
narrative style with language suitable to the character puts across
the quality of her thoughts without damaging their immediacy:

> The raillery of young Delvile . . . had taught her to fear the con-
> structions of the world, and she therefore purposed to keep both
> the surgeon and Mr. Belfield ignorant to whom they were in-
> debted. She was aware, indeed, that . . . that high-spirited and
> unfortunate young man would be extremely hurt to find himself
> thus detected and pursued; but she thought his life too well worth
> preserving to let it be sacrificed to his pride, and her internal con-
> viction of being herself the immediate cause of its present danger,
> gave to her an anxious and restless desire to be herself the means
> of extricating him from it.
>
> (*Cecilia*, III.v)

Burney is already beginning to display one of the major preoccupations of Victorian novelists, like Trollope and George
Eliot, in investigating the relation between a sense of self and the
outside world. Like Cecilia, hundreds of later characters have

been 'taught' by the attitudes of those around them, which in complex ways affect their 'anxious and restless desire' for solutions to their dilemmas.

A very credible mental torment becomes a standard form of poetic justice meted out in Victorian novels, such as Trollope's *The Small House at Allington* (1862–4), in which Crosbie is here getting his just deserts after jilting the heroine in favour of the insufferable daughter of an earl:

> His wife, as his wife, should obey him . . . or else leave him and go her way by herself, leaving him to go his way . . . All his old comforts of course he could not have—nor the old esteem and regard of men . . . And then he remembered how ugly Alexandrina had been this evening, wearing a great tinsel coronet full of false stones . . . She certainly was very plain! So he said to himself, and then he went to bed. I myself am inclined to think that his punishment was sufficiently severe.
>
> (chapter 48)

Such a passage—central to a whole class of Victorian novels— depends upon precedents from Austen's day, though typically the bite and economy are less sharp than with her, for this fiction should engender sympathy with many varieties of erring human imperfection.

Because of a Victorian habit of analysing prose fiction principally in terms of subject-matter, Austen was often regarded as a minor figure, and credited with little influence on subsequent great novelists, even by those, like George Eliot and Henry James, who profited by the techniques which she and her lesser contemporaries had brought to perfection, Trollope alone among important novelists acknowledging his debt. In the 1860s, however, it gradually became more widely accepted that to study everyday behaviour was not necessarily trivial, since, properly conceived, the gestures and minutiae of middle-class social behaviour constituted a 'language of manners' which could be as valid a subject of investigation as literature's perpetual concern, language itself. The ability to make important moral statements about life, within the confines of the drawing-room, was particularly important in an age of heavy middle-class conformity, and most of all necessary when dealing in a socially acceptable way with middle-class women, the most conventionally restricted part of the population. Broadly speaking, Austen perfected the techniques of dramatic character-presentation, socially analysed language, and careful narrative control, which were necessary for one of the principal Victorian subjects—the dilemma of individual moral choice in the bourgeois world.

SIR WALTER SCOTT

In the mid-nineteenth century one read Austen for her 'limited' perfection, but Scott for subject-matter and elevation, it being, Bulwer Lytton proposed, the office of the novelist

> to take man from the low passions, and the miserable troubles of life, into a higher region . . . to excite a generous sorrow at vicissitudes not his own, to raise the passions into sympathy with heroic struggles—and to admit the soul into that serener atmosphere from which it rarely returns to ordinary existence, without some memory or association which ought to enlarge the domain of thought and exalt the motives of action . . .

This elevation of the soul into realms supposedly above the sordid reality of the present was to come about through literature of large, heroic action, through the imaginative participation in the great events of history or through rediscovering the chivalric ideas of another age. Although it is usual today to prefer Scott's treatment of average, unexceptional people caught up in quite recent Scottish history to his grander money-making flights among the kings and dukes of more remote times and places, Victorian readers stressed his amplitude. And the appeal for each individual went deep at a personal level. Not only had Scott greatly raised the status of prose fiction by the importance of his subject-matter in chronicling his country's history, but his work was irreproachably pure, with 'a plain, wholesome, and uncompromising air of morality', so that he was read in many households from which the great eighteenth-century novelists were banned. Consequently large numbers of Victorians grew up with Scott as their greatest early experience in the novel, as did George Eliot, whose 'worship for Scott' was so strong that for the rest of her life it was 'a personal grief, a heart-wound' to hear 'a depreciating or slighting word' about him.

The greatest debt Victorian novelists owed Scott was that he taught them how to understand the place of the individual in history and analyse a person's experience of a given moment in terms of historical change. For the Victorians were more conscious than any previous people of living in an age of rapid change—and they had good reason to be. Industrialisation and capital accumulation aggravated wealth differences and class conflicts. Urbanisation concentrated human misery to an extent hitherto unparalleled and, in the name of industrial, technical and scientific advance, millions were forced to live in conditions in which their employers and 'betters' would not have dreamt of keeping their horses. Seen from a middle-class point of view these were the calamities naturally attending on science and technology, and a dramatic expansion in trade and manufacture, with a consequently great improvement—again as far as the middle class was concerned—in the standard of living and the conveniences of life. Well-maintained toll-roads had been a stimulus to trade and travel, but the railway completely transformed the country in a few decades. Old coaching towns died; new railway towns sprang up. In less than a century the country was altered beyond recognition, not only in the big centres of population but in the remote countryside too. For a large part of the Victorian middle classes change was beneficial and stimulating, but it brought a burden of social guilt with it. Rapid change breeds alarm and insecurity even among those whom it does not reduce to misery; consequently a widespread Victorian middle-class syndrome was a simultaneous excitement at and approval of 'progress', and a yearning after a more secure state of things, attended by less guilt and uncertainty. Hence there was a nostalgia for the past—or rather for a past that existed in the harried nineteenth-century imagination.

All this is to say that the Victorians experienced their own time as history. In this they were the heirs of Defoe, with his social and economic explanations of life, and could look back on the final destruction of Augustan optimism, from an age when industrial and political revolutions had overtaken the world, and the old static models of hierarchic perfection had become unthinkable. Many Victorian novelists—Dickens, Thackeray, Trollope and George Eliot among them—set out as historians to record their own societies, and for the first time in English fiction apply the notions of historicism to the present moment. The study of historical process as a means of understanding the present state of things and the flux in which it was caught was developed in Edinburgh by thinkers who found themselves in a culturally ambiguous position in the latter part of the eighteenth century. Speaking Scots but writing a 'standard' English for the larger English market, celebrating a Scotland and its culture which had been deprived of independence and nationhood first when James VI moved south to rule and enjoy their richer neighbour and 'auld enemy' in 1603, and then when the Act of Union of 1707 abolished the Scottish parliament, the Edinburgh literati were forcibly aware of history as a process in which the individual lives and dies. Their position was ambivalent. They were not watching a national decline and fall only, because the country now subsisted on the trade which the self-same Act of Union had opened up. Edinburgh as capital city could indulge in nostalgia for past glories, but Glasgow merchants could enjoy present growth and, like Bailie Nicol Jarvie in Scott's *Rob Roy*, look forward to future flourishing. Scott himself reflected the prevailing cultural ambivalence, at once celebrating old Scotland in verse and prose, and welcoming George IV on his 1822 visit to Edinburgh, which started the grand roup of national character and lands to the English throughout the nineteenth century.

Like many of his contemporaries Scott was deeply influenced by the books and lectures of Edinburgh thinkers, such as Adam Ferguson (1723–1816) and Dugald Stewart (1753–1828). Ferguson's *An Essay on the History of Civil Society* (1767), for example, taught that human life was inconceivable without society, and traced the development of different social and political systems through the ages in terms of national conflict and the clash of interest-groups, to show that the resulting social order expressed 'that medium and composition which contending parties have forced one another to adopt'. Scott's Scottish novels seek to explain the world by describing the life of private individuals in the conflicts out of which early-nineteenth-century Scotland was made, from the seventeenth-century religious wars and the '45 rebellion to the scarcely less violent power struggles between the old aristocracy and the new bourgeoisie.

Scott's teachers belonged to the school of 'common sense' and, in view of the novelist's use of folk-wisdom or his structuring of a great novel like *The Heart of Midlothian* (1818) around the heroic resolves, actions and reactions of a lower-class character like Jeanie Deans, it is significant that Ferguson, in his frequent appeals to 'common sense', takes the term to cover what a 'peasant' would think. As E. S. Dallas remarked on looking back from 1858, the

> leading principle [of Scottish philosophy] is an appeal to 'common sense;' an emphatic assertion that to all those questions about which the metaphysicians wrangle . . . there is absolutely no solution save that which is rendered by the vulgar consciousness and the universal belief of mankind . . .

Scott was a supreme exponent of 'the vulgar consciousness'. No novelist had ever had such direct theoretical encouragement to centre an examination of the world in ordinary and not exceptional characters, and to take his lower-class people as seriously as their 'betters'.

The ease with which moral philosophers—from Hume, Ferguson and Adam Smith to Stewart and then Mackintosh—moved from the study of 'human nature' to politics, economics and history is a characteristic of the Scottish school, and made their work of immediate importance to a practical student of life in society, like Scott. Dugald Stewart, for example, guided the thought of generations of students and more distant admirers—major statesmen and many of the greatest British thinkers of the first half of the nineteenth century among them—and it is natural that a fiction formed by the ideas of the Scottish philosophers should find ready acceptance in the Victorian age, which was trying to understand itself by principles originally derived from those of Scott's actual teachers and mentors.

In most of Scott's best novels, history is seen from the point of view of an average sort of protagonist: someone scarcely raised above the ordinary run of humanity by gifts, understanding or virtue, and yet able to stand as typical of a particular social class at a definite period. Through being placed in a problematic position, like the Englishman Edward Waverley on adopting the Stuart cause in 1745, or Henry Morton in *Old Mortality* with his loyalties dangerously divided between the Royalists and the Covenanters, the mediocre hero becomes the register of the principal feelings and motivations attending great historical events. To develop the situation to the full the protagonist is often made to vacillate endlessly, and can risk turning out, as Scott himself unfairly said of Waverley, as 'a sneaking piece of imbecility'. Scott, however, does not merely present individuals, but has a more generous scope, displaying the ways in which ordinary people are affected by the great movements of history, and hence in effect taking the development of a whole nation or area of society as his subject.

His deep imaginative understanding of historical processes makes him supreme among historical novelists in English, and the example to the greatest in other languages too, for Tolstoy is using a method like Scott's in *War and Peace* (1863–9) when he exploits Pierre as his key figure. The novel has often favoured the unheroic protagonist who could be a representative of ordinary mortals, from Lesage's Gil Blas or Smollett's Roderick Random to Flaubert's *homme moyen sensuel* and so to the modern anti-hero; but it was Scott who first placed this mediocre personage in the stream of history by presenting his dilemmas as part-and-parcel of the political and cultural clashes of his age.

Scott's technique was extended by Victorian novelists to apply to the outwardly less violent revolutions of the nineteenth century. The decisions facing many of Trollope's or George Eliot's characters not only involve their individual destinies but exemplify a whole area of social or political concern, as in the case of the hero's political choices in Trollope's *Phineas Finn* (1867–9) or Lydgate's professional problems in George Eliot's *Middlemarch* (1871–2). The hero was taken down off his stilts and levelled with the rest of the world to serve as a sympathetic moral receptacle, with the result that the very everyday quality which seemed to Dr Johnson an encouragement to vice became with the Victorians the key to realistic moral teaching, reflecting a change from the habit of judging individual morality against Augustan absolutes towards a more relativistic investigation of social morality in terms of context and circumstances, stemming from the sort of inquiry Scott started in *The Heart of Midlothian* into how far social legality and individual righteousness could be made consistent.

Scott's own conflicting feelings on many of the historical events he presented—such as the '45, with which as a supporter of his 'Fat Friend' George IV he should not logically have sympathised —enabled him to present opposing cases unusually fairly. In *Rob Roy* he presents a cultural conflict with dual sympathy, through a narrator Frank Osbaldistone who does not himself properly belong to this clash between mercantile Glasgow and the proud Highland independence which will not 'bide the coercion of gude braid-claith about [the] hinderlans; let a be breeks o' freestone, and garters o' iron'. The struggle which destroys the star-cross'd lovers of *The Bride of Lammermoor* (1819) is fought out between the old aristocracy and the rising men of power, between 'equity' and 'law', and proprietorial rights as opposed to mere possession. As a lawyer Scott saw the Ashton's Whig case for property and order, but his Tory sympathies and his imaginative grasp of tradition through folklore and folk language led him to write with extra *brio* of the old order, even when standing himself on the side of the new.

Scott's reputation as a social historian rests on his ability to produce an authentic voice from the people to express the feelings of a whole class or generation, and when the social dimensions are lost or obscured—as those of *The Bride of Lammermoor* largely are in Donizetti's operatic version, *Lucia di Lammermoor*—historical fiction sinks to costume drama and tragedy is reduced to melodrama, as social conflict is replaced by the mere clash of individual wills. Only a full understanding of folk-tales, beliefs and customs could produce the typical mouthpieces through which Scott presents his different segments of society. Similarly with language; to achieve a broad social perspective, the novelist must, like Scott, have at his command a language which really corresponds to that of the people whom he is presenting, and is not a stage-conventional comic dialect which, quite apart from its inherent falseness, is designed to give readers a sense of superiority and distances them from the 'low' characters, who instead of being full social representatives can be no more than one-dimensional 'secondary' figures. The range of colloquial Scots in the Waverley Novels is exceptional, and hardly equalled except by Dickens's command of the varieties of Cockney and Home Counties' dialect.

Scott found precedents for the use of a 'social voice' in presenting the fortunes of a house or family, as opposed to an individual. In *The Castle of Otranto* Walpole had employed prophecies and what he called 'Shakesperian' secondary characters for this purpose, and Scott does something similar in a novel like *The Bride of Lammermoor*, but with the secondary characters no longer simply absurd and with the supernaturalism incorporated as folk-belief to give an air of fatalism without an actual ghostly presence. Maria Edgeworth's account of rural Irish decay in *Castle Rackrent* (1800) also encouraged Scott to analyse his characters' fates in terms of economic and social relations which had operated over generations—an approach he adopted the more readily because he saw in her Ireland a worse case of the same ills which had afflicted Scotland since 1603.

Besides transmitting these social facilities to his Victorian admirers, Scott gave novelists a new kind of confidence by adopting a narrative voice which, in contrast to his predecessors', is quite unembarrassed by the existence of the narrative. The fiction of Richardson, Fielding and Sterne constantly needs to explain the strange fact of appearing on the printed page at all, but while Scott uses numbers of fictional authors, story-tellers and commentators, these are largely brief inductional devices to smooth the reader's way into the fiction and at the same time semi-humorously conceal the identity of 'the Author of Waverley'; the stream of narrative flows thereafter uncomplicated by the aesthetic problems which obsessed the great eighteenth-century novelists. In this respect Scott was the most straightforward of narrative stylists, and his directness simply involved the reader in the sheer delight of story-telling in a way which most Victorian novelists were pleased to emulate.

He has many unhappy *longueurs*, such as the openings of *The Antiquary* or *Rob Roy*, which are very slow because—like many succeeding Victorians—he starts ponderously with setting, background information and character-sketches before launching into story. It is understandable that his manner of 'extempore' writing fell into discredit with the aesthetically-minded generation of the late nineteenth century who had read French authors like Flaubert and knew things about composition with which the Wizard of the North had not concerned himself. So, despite his truly international reputation and his unique influence on the Victorians, Scott had to be excluded from the late-century calendar of aesthetic saints. But he was none the less the most celebrated British novelist in his own country and throughout Europe for almost a century.

CHAPTER 7

Dickens and the Literature of London

A great deal of Victorian literature shows an urgent effort to come to terms with radically new and rapidly changing conditions of life, such as the growth of what Carlyle called 'that monstrous tuberosity of Civilised Life, the Capital of England'. For many generations writers had fallen under the spell of London, and its fascination can be seen in the variety of human types Ben Jonson exhibited in his city comedies, or in the love-hate of Pope's *Dunciad*, or Dr Johnson's well-known comment that 'when a man is tired of London, he is tired of life; for there is in London all that life can afford'. A commonplace eighteenth-century view of London was that it was stimulating beyond compare, but dangerous, always liable to riot and commotion, for in it, as Dr Johnson wrote, 'now a rabble rages, now a fire'. This enduring ambivalence towards the city was summed up by William Cowper in *The Task* (1785), who saw in London

> Much that I love, and more that I admire,
> And all that I abhor . . .
>
> (III, ll. 838–9)

London was a microcosm of the world, displaying 'human nature' in all its divinely appointed variety, through all social conditions with their inevitable inequalities. A visual satirist like Hogarth could show the whole condition of humanity everywhere, in his London scenes, drawing his picture from the most vital and concentrated model of human life available.

Shelley appears to be in this tradition when he draws on the implicit imagery of the previous century for his comparison:

> Hell is a city much like London—
> A populous and smoky city
> (*Peter Bell the Third*, III.i)

but he, like Blake, recognises the economic and environmental determinants in this urban world, and attributes what he sees to social conditions and not just the operation of a generalised 'human nature'. As the nineteenth century progressed, social and economic factors received more prominent attention, and during the century the metropolis became so overwhelming that it had to be seen as a monster which destroyed its victims, like a minotaur at the centre of the urban labyrinth, consuming virgins by the thousand every year, or in Shelley's words

> . . . that great sea, whose ebb and flow
> At once is deaf and loud, and on the shore
> Vomits it wrecks, and still howls on for more.
> ('Letter to Maria Gisborne', ll. 193–5)

Already in the 1720s Defoe described London as

a prodigy of buildings, that nothing in the world does, or ever did, equal it, except old Rome in Trajan's time, when the walls were fifty miles in compass, and the number of inhabitants six million eight hundred thousand souls.

> (*A Tour through the Whole Island of Great
> Britain*, 1724–6, PEL, p286)

By 1848, said Leigh Hunt

every village which was in the immediate and even remote neighbourhood of London, and was quite distinct from one another at
the beginning of the reign of George the Third, is now almost, if
not quite, joined with it, including Highgate and Hampstead . . .
on the north, Norwood on the south, Turnham Green and
Parson's Green on the west, and Laytonstone [sic] on the east.

(*The Town*)

The richest, largest city became—like New York in our century—
the greatest administrative problem and it is no wonder that, in
reaction, William Morris summoned up a Utopian vision of the
city:

> Forget six counties overhung with smoke,
> Forget the snorting steam and piston stroke,
> . . .
> And dream of London, small, and white, and clean,
> The clear Thames bordered by its gardens green . . .
>
> (*The Earthly Paradise*, 1870, Prologue,
> 'The Wanderers', ll. 1–6)

Because of its size and variety the metropolis was 'a nation, not
a city' to Disraeli, and to Emerson on his visits from America in
1833 and 1847 it was 'the epitome of our times, and the Rome of
to-day'. On the credit side this made 'the Metropolis . . . a complete CYCLOPAEDIA' for Pierce Egan, and for Hazlitt 'the only
place in which the child grows completely up into the man'. Size
gave anonymity, for, as the comic writer Robert Surtees put it in
1851, 'In London nobody cares what his neighbours do. The only
man really known in London is the Duke of Wellington.' On the
other hand, the gulfs between people and the terrible isolation
produced by the town were recognised by arrivals from outside
who, like Wordsworth, could not understand

> . . . how men lived
> Even next-door neighbours, as we say, yet still
> Strangers, and knowing not each other's names.
>
> (*The Prelude*, 1805, VII, ll. 117–20)

The very qualities which made London a dazzling spectacle made it the cause of the greatest human desolation. As the popular Victorian preacher Charles Spurgeon wrote, 'A great city is a great wilderness. There is no such absolute loneliness as that which many have felt in London.'

A vivid realisation of this human alienation and its roots in economic relations came to the Swedish poet, Erik Gustaf Geijer, when he first arrived in London in 1809 and found himself

> lonely among a million human beings . . . I have never had a more vivid conception of a desert than at the moment when I first found myself in the midst of the most populous city in Europe. I experienced for the first time quite vividly the sensation of being a *stranger*. Among savages the word means the same as *enemy*. But even that is a human relationship. Here to the whole world I was mortally indifferent, except for my postilion until he got his payment, and for my hotelier so long as he was waiting for his. Oddly enough, money is merely the token of commodities. How much is a human being worth then, when he is but a token of the token?—a shadow of the shadow?

Such loneliness in the crowd, coupled with ignorance as to the meaning of the activities of those around, encourages people to replace true understanding by mystery and speculation, in the fashion of Silas Wegg, the one-legged street-vendor in Dickens's *Our Mutual Friend* (1864–5), who not knowing enough facts erects his own imaginary version of life in the house he stands outside. A reliable interpreter of the signs to be seen in London was called for. The comic perambulations of Tom, Jerry and Logic through scenes of low life in Pierce Egan's *Life in London* (1821) exposed new aspects of the metropolis for readers' curiosity and amusement, but it was Dickens who most fully developed the literature of the new urban scene, so that the journalistic pieces he gathered together as *Sketches by Boz* (1836) held a special place in public affection for decades, as unique keys to the modern world.

In the *Sketches* Dickens tries out the full complexity of response to London life which is a necessary precondition for his later

fiction. His persona, Boz, stands in a long line of strolling ob-
servers, of whom the best earlier example is found in Gay's *Trivia:
or, the Art of Walking the Streets of London* (1716), as a sympathetic,
charitable recorder, happy to remain detached while watching the
human pageant. Boz, too, though lacking the exquisite sensibility
of the later Parisian stroller or *flâneur*, responds instantly to every
passing sight. In many of the pieces he is a disengaged walker
through the streets of London, rarely involved in what he sees,
and adopting nonce attitudes which govern his approach to each
scene in turn and which can conflict because of his fundamental
ambivalence towards the phenomena he records, finding them at
once fascinating and disturbing, full of human possibilities yet
morally appalling. For example, he exposes dishonest cab-drivers
and omnibus 'cads', but treats the inconveniences of London life
with amused tolerance, mingled with pride; for the problems of
metropolitan life are part of its charm and assume a positive force
as a familiar substitute for a true understanding of the social web.
As a reaction to his human alienation, the observer animates objects
he encounters, so that old clothes for sale in Monmouth Street can
have more vitality than actual people in the street. He can be
compassionate, as he is in his description of 'Shabby-Genteel
People', but is only emotionally roused at family scenes or the
plight of the young prostitutes in 'The Prisoners' Van'.

His 'superior' attitude to his material is not based on a socially
secure status—he apparently lives a very modest middle-class life
in reduced circumstances in the suburbs—but on a close knowledge
of the way London works. Yet the city is a mystery too big even
for him, and he is the interpreter of a world which is too complex
to be completely understood. So, at the domestic level, his response to urban life is to present a picture of family unity,
especially reunion at Christmastime, as a myth to hold up against
the dehumanised life of the modern working world. And, of
course, he is funny, at the expense of hypocrisy and petty tyranny
or from a sheer delight in the ludicrous. In very many ways the
Sketches by Boz are an auspicious beginning to a great career, in

large part devoted to analysing forms of awareness in the modern world.

One phenomenon demanding the attention of writers was the town crowd, which was seen in its characteristically modern form for the first time in nineteenth-century London, where the irresistible streams of people inspired the idea of power and purpose, while the sheer mass of humanity could raise fears of loss of identity, but a sense too of mystery, which might be gratifying in its own right. One response to urban alienation was to try to master the intricacies of the city as a machine, and Edgar Allan Poe's narrator in 'Man of the Crowd' (1841) is obeying a characteristic impulse of modern man as investigator or detective when he follows a stranger through the streets, alleys, markets and pubs of London in pursuit of a solution to the enigma of the city. The narrator, an American and hence significantly an outsider, describes the rush-hour crowd flowing past the coffee-shop window where he is ensconced one autumn evening:

> . . . by the time the lamps were well lighted, two dense and continuous tides of population were rushing past the door . . . By far the greater number of those who went by had a satisfied business-like demeanour, and seemed to be thinking only of making their way through the press. Their brows were knit, and their eyes rolled quickly; when pushed against by fellow-wayfarers they evinced no symptom of impatience, but adjusted their clothes and hurried on. Others . . . were restless in their movements, had flushed faces, and talked and gesticulated to themselves, as feeling in solitude on account of the very denseness of the company around.

To the unimpassioned observer there was something strange, even insane, in such crowd-behaviour as Poe described, and yet this was only one aspect of the way in which description of the city could not be distinguished from fantasy, since the appearance it presented was as startling as any poetic flight, while fact had an inherent tendency to become symbol or allegory. In a description of Cheapside on a rainy day in *Sketches by Boz*, Dickens showed

London as a strange, secretive and potentially dangerous place:

> Cabs whisked about, with the 'fare' as carefully boxed up behind
> two glazed calico curtains as any mysterious picture in any one of
> Mrs. Radcliffe's castles; omnibus horses smoked like steam-
> engines . . .
>
> ('A Bloomsbury Christening', Everyman, p425)

Coupling sensational gothic to the modern image of the steam-
engine is typical of Dickens's synthetic power and by no means
gratuitous. The dangers of Mrs Radcliffe's *Mysteries of Udolpho* are
realised in a comic parallel which illustrates how urban man is
powerless in a hostile environment, when Mr Nicodemus Dumps
is 'kidnapped' by an omnibus conductor and carried helplessly
past Drury Lane where he wants to be set down.

The highest development of the city scene as fact and fantasy
is the famous opening passage of *Bleak House* (1852-3):

> London. Michaelmas Term lately over, and the Lord Chancellor
> sitting in Lincoln's Inn Hall. Implacable November weather. As
> much mud in the streets, as if the waters had but newly retired from
> the face of the earth, and it would not be wonderful to meet a
> Megalosaurus, forty feet long or so, waddling like an elephantine
> lizard up Holborn Hill.

Here Dickens brilliantly concentrates an idea which had earlier
amused Leigh Hunt, who imagined a remote era when 'some
unknown monster, mammoth or behemoth, howled in the twi-
light over the ocean solitude now called London', or an elephant
'recreated himself . . . on the site of the Chapter Coffee house'.
Dickens intensifies the strangeness by bringing it even closer to
the everyday, to fit the opening of a novel of social criticism,
which is built around mystery, the labyrinth, and surprising
interconnections and revelations, and in which an early fictional
police detective plays his part—for detective and mystery stories
grow naturally out of the incomprehensible strangeness of the
London world. It is no coincidence that Wilkie Collins's Woman

in White (1860) is first seen in a melodramatic attitude, 'pointing to the dark cloud over London', the home of mystery; for it is essential to Collins's art to show that 'the butcher, the baker, and the tax-gatherer, are not the only credible realities' in mid-Victorian Britain. As one critic put it, 'Proximity is, indeed, one great element of sensation.' Dickens's achievement can never be classified within any one conventional mode of fiction, but among its many aspects *Bleak House* shows the full enigma of modern life which lies at the root of the detective fiction of then and now.

The various characters in *Bleak House*—from the wretchedly poor and ignorant crossing-sweeper, Jo, through the self-effacing middle-class narrator of half the story, Esther Summerson, to the wealthy, upper-class Sir Leicester and Lady Dedlock—all seemingly inhabit different social worlds, and the central enigma to be worked out through a complex plot of mystery and revelation is put directly to the reader, in chapter 16, by the omniscient narrator who shares the story-telling with Esther:

> What connexion can there be, between the place in Lincolnshire, the house in town, the Mercury in powder, and the whereabout of Jo the outlaw with the broom . . . ? What connexion can there have been between many people in the innumerable histories of this world, who, from opposite sides of great gulfs, have, nevertheless, been very curiously brought together!
>
> (PEL, p272)

The answer is partly found through the revelation of blood relationships where least expected, although not only for melodrama or the pleasure of scenes of dramatic recognition in themselves, but as a moral statement about the nature of society. It may be comfortable for the well-to-do to close their eyes and ears to the existence of Jo and the slums, but nevertheless, as Thomas Carlyle had taught the world in his *Past and Present* and *Latter-Day Pamphlets*, the whole of society is bound together by hidden links which it ignores at its peril. Jo gives Esther small-pox, for example, and shows by this the moral and physical contagions which horrifically tie the world together. Dickens converts fact into symbol, and realistic action into allegory, in a warning of imminent social collapse which can only be averted by radically remedying social conditions.

The world of *Bleak House* is shrouded in fog—realistic fog but symbolic, too, of moral and political obfuscation, the miasma of disease and ignorance, and the scandalously slow operation of the law which consumes the health and wealth of many of the characters in the interminable case of Jarndyce and Jarndyce, that has been fought in Chancery for decades, to the profit of generations of parasitic lawyers. At the very opening of the novel, the Lord Chancellor is introduced like a surrealistic vision from Pope's *Dunciad*, enthroned with a foggy halo about his head. But the day will come when the institutions of the country will destroy themselves in a cataclysm prefigured in the macabre 'spontaneous combustion' of Krook, who is a burlesque Lord Chancellor in a burlesque Court of Chancery.

With its extended symbolism, morally significant plotting and controlled humour and pathos, *Bleak House* displays Dickens's powers at their height, and includes his most advanced experiment in narrative method too. A maze can be viewed with understanding from above, or experienced as a puzzle from within, and Dickens adapts his narrative to give this dual perspective on the labyrinth of the modern world. Half is recounted in the present tense by an omniscient voice, and half—interspersed among the rest—is written in the past tense by Esther Summerson, who is no cleverer and has no more privileged knowledge of the world than anyone else, so that as the story proceeds the first narrator gradually reveals his secrets, while the second makes a journey of discovery, and the complex world has been explained at the end from within and from without.

Dickens had an impressive list of successes behind him by the time he had carried his art to this kind of perfection. His first novel, *Posthumous Papers of the Pickwick Club* (1836–7), more or less grew out of a commission to provide letter-press for a series of comic prints showing a group of cockney sportsmen in ludicrous difficulties, but he soon broke free from the constraints of this scheme, and subordinated the illustrations to the text. Once he had discarded the ponderous apparatus of the Pickwick Club and introduced Sam Weller as a down-to-earth humorous counterpart to the benevolent and idealistic Mr Pickwick, he was able to develop his characters and situations into a kind of quixotic pattern, through a hilarious sequence of episodic adventures, until a firmer plot-line sprang out of Mrs Bardell's breach-of-promise case against Mr Pickwick, which results in his stay in the Fleet Prison. As befits a comic protagonist, Mr Pickwick bounces safely out of his misfortunes, but the dark side of the world has been exposed, and the evil not defeated.

In the course of the book Dickens tries out most of his resources of humour and horror—the latter largely encapsulated in a number of in-set stories—and exercises the stylistic gifts which his love of Smollett encouraged him to exploit. There is an exuberant, almost prodigal outpouring of talent in this early work, which in terms of liveliness, humour and sheer attractiveness he never surpassed. What develops in his later work is the application of these gifts to coherent, carefully controlled ends. Take the speech of Mr Jingle in *Pickwick Papers*, for example, which is obviously inspired by Smollett and Holcroft:

> 'Heads, heads—take care of your heads!' cried the loquacious stranger, as they came out under the low archway, which in those days formed the entrance to the coach-yard. 'Terrible place—dangerous work—other day—five children—mother—tall lady, eating sandwiches—forgot the arch—crash—knock—children look round—mother's head off—sandwich in her hand—no mouth to put it in—head of a family off—shocking, shocking!'
>
> (chapter 2, PEL, pp78–9)

Beyond suiting a comic villain, this style exists largely for its own sake, but when—to choose one example among a hundred—Dickens creates a characteristic style for Flora Finching twenty years later in *Little Dorrit* (1855–7), it is in order to express her as a 'moral mermaid', living half in her middle-aged present and half in her youthful past when she was in love with Arthur Clennam:

> '. . . good gracious Arthur!—pray excuse me—old habit—Mr Clennam far more proper—what a country [i.e. China] to live in for so long a time, and with so many lanterns and umbrellas too how very dark and wet the climate ought to be and no doubt actually is, and the sums of money that must be made by both those two trades where everybody carries them and hangs them everywhere, the little shoes too and the feet screwed back in infancy is quite surprising, what a traveller you are!'
>
> (chapter 13, PEL, pp 193–4)

The gain is in the *use* Dickens makes of speech-styles, not in his skill in rendering characteristic utterances in which he is unsurpassed from his earliest work onwards, so that in this respect only Shakespeare and James Joyce can be mentioned in the same breath.

Pickwick Papers was an important exercise in part-publication, coming out in nineteen monthly numbers, with a final double part for the price of one, Dickens being the most successful novelist to appear in this way, which became the dominant mode of publication until the 1860s. He quickly established a unique relationship with his readers, and during his career was often able to respond to public reaction and criticism as his novels progressed, as well as locking his fictional chronology into the actual calendar year, so that the Christmas scenes in *Pickwick*, for example, occur at appropriate times. He was the supreme serialist, able to adapt from monthly parts to weekly periodical publication as occasion demanded, simultaneously creating books as wholes and as carefully structured episodes; so that at one end of the scale his suspense could be so brilliantly built up that crowds lined the quayside in New York to learn from an arriving ship whether Little Nell was dead yet in *The Old Curiosity Shop* (1840–1), while at a subtler level a masterpiece like *Great Expectations* (1860–1) is not only one of the best-constructed novels in the language, but displays in every one of its thirty-six weekly episodes a judicious balance of light and shade, building up in each case to an unforced moment of tension.

Pickwick Papers was still coming out when Dickens began his next serial, *Oliver Twist* (1838–9), in which he appeared for the first time as a social campaigner, attacking the inhumanity of the 1834 Poor Law under which Oliver suffers, and the petty tyranny of the beadles, magistrates and workhouse guardians. All his life he was to take up specific causes in his fiction, such as the abominations of the Yorkshire schools satirised in Dotheboys Hall in *Nicholas Nickleby* (1838–9), and sanitation, housing and education in many of his other books, together with attacks on targets as various as administrative corruption, incompetence and nepotism, or sabbatarianism which he thought aimed to make the working population's one rest-day of the week as miserable as the other six.

Other writers fought similar campaigns through their fiction. Bulwer Lytton boasted that his *Paul Clifford* (1830) had 'had its share in the wise and great relaxation of our Criminal Code', while Charles Kingsley's *Alton Locke* (1850) was an influential exposé of tailoring sweat-shops, and slum conditions in St Giles, one of the worst areas of London. In *It's Never too Late to Mend* (1856), Charles Reade, a friend and collaborator of Dickens's, attacked brutal prison discipline, basing his case on the suicide of a fifteen-year-old prisoner in 1853, because of illegal and excessive punishment, and in *Hard Cash* (1863) he described the bad conditions prevailing in many lunatic asylums, and revealed how, as was made public in the real case of Fletcher *v*. Fletcher, sane persons could quite easily be confined in them by unscrupulous relatives who would then enjoy their income.

Public ignorance stood in the way of reform on all fronts, and radicals willingly adopted fiction as their vehicle. To meet the sceptical view that, in *The Times*'s words, 'Eccentric fact makes improbable fiction, and improbable fiction is not impressive', Reade explained that fact was indeed stranger than fiction:

> I feign probabilities; I record improbabilities: the former are conjectures, the latter truths: mixed they make a thing not so true as Gospel nor so false as History: viz., Fiction.
>
> When I startle you most, think twice before you disbelieve me. What able deceiver aims at shocking credulity? Distrust rather my oily probabilities.
>
> (Introduction to *Autobiography of a Thief*, 1858)

This passage is not only a 'clue' to Reade's own writing, but a general statement about the nature of the fiction of the period which presented the public with new or unpalatable ideas. Nevertheless 'good facts may be bad art', but what Dickens drew from topical news fitted into a total imaginative vision of the life of the metropolis, often assuming a symbolic significance in the process, like the collapse of Mrs Clennam's house in *Little Dorrit* when the secrets it contains have been revealed. In the fiction of lesser writers, the amalgam often fails, and the result at worst can be a hotch-potch of love-story, documentary and melodrama. For his part, Dickens could accommodate anything, however 'eccentric', into his lively and grotesque comic world.

His greatest strength in social description not only derives from his knowledge of London, which like Sam Weller's 'was extensive and peculiar', but from the way in which right from *Sketches by Boz* he contrived to identify himself with the whole life of the capital. Even when there is no clearly personalised narrator like 'Boz', the authorial voice still indicates a relish and involvement in what it describes, and by contrast most other writers are comparative outsiders, leading the reader conscientiously into the back-streets and alleys. When dealing with London, Dickens is never a tourist and the reader is placed in the midst of an inhabited fictional city, not treated to a guided excursion. He can also deal with a wide social range, and does not concentrate solely on the criminal and semi-criminal classes, as novelists of the 1830s did in the main. The nightmare labyrinth of the under-world in *Oliver Twist* is an exception in Dickens's work in as much as it dominates the book, although a similar atmosphere is evoked as a subsidiary part of most of the later novels. An exclusive attention to criminality forbids a broad view of the urban life of most of the population. On these grounds alone Dickens is the greatest poet of Victorian London.

He spent some years before he succeeded in integrating his diverse perceptions into one coherent vision. His earliest novels were largely based on the rambling, episodic structure employed by his favourite Smollett. A variety of scenes in different social and geographical areas could easily be linked together, with the risk that the novel might fall apart at the seams, as *Nicholas Nickleby* certainly does. There is a tension in all this early work between the loose eighteenth-century episodic structure and the quite different demands of melodramatic plotting. (Dickens was, and remained all his life, deeply attached to current theatrical forms, as spectator, writer and amateur actor.) But all the time he was exercising arts which were essential to his later achievement.

The Old Curiosity Shop is structured like a fairy-tale, polarised between the ogre, Quilp, and the innocent Little Nell—the former being the source of all the demonic energy of the book and the latter what mathematicians eloquently term the 'sink', in this case Quilp's intended victim and the receptacle of the reader's sentimental tears. Yet even an obviously unsatisfactory novel like this has greatnesses, such as Little Nell's allegorical journey from the town to the country with her grandfather, passing through the hell of the industrial Midlands, lit up at night by weird blast-furnace fires and disturbed by Chartist demonstrations, to the unearthly peace of the crumbling village churchyard beyond. In this novel, too, Dickens presents one of his most potent mytho-poeic characters in the person of Dick Swiveller, who creates around him a world to satisfy his own imaginative longings, just as Dickens himself was doing for his large readership.

Martin Chuzzlewit (1843–4) is a great advance, although endangered by Dickens's need to send Martin to America to improve the sales which were lagging dangerously, but revived by his hilarious and biting satire on American public life and character. This is nevertheless the first book which he structured around one clear, explicit aim: to display selfishness and hypocrisy in action in various interlocking levels of society, but personified principally in Mr Pecksniff, the 'Great Abstraction', who is seen dropping a typical paste-gem of morality as he and his daughters settle themselves inside a coach on a cold day, with the satisfactory feeling that the outside passengers are not as warm as they are:

> And this, he said, was quite natural, and a very beautiful arrangement; not confined to coaches, but extending itself into many social ramifications. 'For' (he observed), 'if every one were warm and well-fed, we should lose the satisfaction of admiring the fortitude with which certain conditions of men bear cold and hunger. And if we were no better off than anybody else, what would become of our sense of gratitude, which,' said Mr Pecksniff with tears in his eyes, as he shook his fist at a beggar who wanted to get up behind, 'is one of the holiest feelings of our common nature.'
>
> (chapter 8, PEL, p174)

Dickens originally wished to underline his moral by a motto on the title-page which was to read: 'Your homes the scene, yourselves the actors, here!' Other counsels prevailed, but from now on his intention of bringing such lessons home to his readers was paramount.

A pause between major novels—he had been hard-pressed since 1836—allowed him to consolidate his gains, and experiment with new modes of incorporating his diverse impulses into an artistically coherent whole, in *The Christmas Books* of 1843–8, which successfully exploited symbolic form and nursery-tale structure as the vehicle for a social message. He was now ready for his first mature masterpiece, *Dombey and Son* (1846–8), in which he continues his investigations into the moral and economic bases of behaviour, dealing now not with individuals or institutions alone but ideologies, in a way which looks forward to his all-out attack, in *Hard Times* (1854), on Utilitarianism and its obsession with facts not people. The dominant vice in *Dombey and Son* is Mr Dombey's pride, which prohibits him from any of the normal human cares and loves, but is finally broken when his old-fashioned merchant-firm is overtaken by the rapid change which is seen transforming the world of the novel as the action takes place. Dombey himself experiences a conversion like Scrooge's in *A Christmas Carol*, and in more ways than one the union of realistic and mythic approaches to the world in *Dombey and Son* can be traced back to *The Christmas Books*.

It is in *Dombey* that Dickens first uses social fact and symbol in an extended fashion, in particular to put across the equation of physical with moral disease which Carlyle was preaching to the world, and his Carlylean rhetoric is at its most powerful, as he boldly castigates the public:

> Look round upon the world of odious sights . . . at the lightest mention of which humanity revolts, and dainty delicacy living in the next street, stops her ears, and lisps 'I don't believe it!' Breathe the polluted air, foul with every impurity that is poisonous to health and life . . . Vainly attempt to think of any simple plant . . . that, set in this foetid bed, could have its natural growth . . . And then, calling up some ghastly child, with stunted form and wicked face, hold forth on its unnatural sinfulness, and lament its being, so early, far away from Heaven—but think a little of its having been conceived, and born and bred, in Hell!
>
> (chapter 47, PEL, P737)

This is forceful homily, but the gain in dramatic power and biting humour in *Bleak House* is striking in comparison, when the unctuous Mr Chadband is actually seen haranguing Jo, the crossing-sweeper, for the improvement of his listeners.

Public health was only one of Dickens's many social interests, but will serve to illustrate his method. While *Dombey* was appearing, Britain was threatened with a new attack of cholera, which had succeeded in frightening the government of the day into some tardy public-health legislation and the appointment of yet one more in a long string of royal commissions on the Health of the Metropolis. Dickens was writing while the enlightened minority were waiting in fear for an attack worse than the one which had killed 6,800 Londoners in 1832–3. Urgent action was called for, the day of national fasting and penance on 6 February 1832 having done little to alleviate the previous outbreak. The imagery of disease in *Dombey* therefore carries with it the inescapable warning of complete social disaster:

> ... if the noxious particles that rise from vitiated air were palpable to the sight, we should see them lowering in a dense black cloud ... and rolling slowly on to corrupt the better portions of a town. But if the moral pestilence that rises with them, and ... is inseparable from them, could be made discernible too, how terrible the revelation! Then should we see depravity, impiety, drunkenness, theft, murder ... creeping on, to blight the innocent and spread contagion among the pure. Then should we see how the same poisoned fountains that flow into our hospitals and lazar-houses, inundate the jails, and make the convict-ships swim deep, ... and over-run vast continents with crime.
>
> (PEL, P738)

Dickens continues his homily with a passage reminiscent of the strategies of *The Christmas Books*:

> Oh for a good spirit who would take the house-tops off ... and show a Christian people what dark shapes issue from amidst their homes, to swell the retinue of the Destroying Angel as he moves among them!
>
> (PEL, P 738)

Scrooge's one-night conversion from misanthropy to benevolence has been expanded into a social programme and, while it is true that in his plotting Dickens too often relies on the spirit of individual humanity—*la philosophie de Noël*, as it has been called—his mature work presents the full social dimensions of the problems he confronts, in the hope that men might be 'delayed no more by stumbling-blocks of their own making . . . [and] would then apply themselves . . . to make the world a better place!' (PEL, pp738–9). Dickens's homily is eloquent, but it is perhaps too obvious that the author is climbing into his pulpit, and the counterbalance between experience from within the maze and explanation from without it is far more subtly achieved by the dual narrative of *Bleak House* five years later.

Though, as *The Times* remarked, 'The cholera is the best of all sanitary reformers', social measures continued to be too slight and too late. It was no exaggeration to say in 1852 that 'the present condition of this huge metropolis exhibits the most extraordinary anomaly in England. Abounding in wealth and intelligence, by far the greater part of it is yet absolutely without any municipal government whatever.' In the summer of 1854 cholera struck London again, and in one area of Soho, only about 250 yards wide, over 500 people died in ten days, the only pump in the neighbourhood having become polluted. In the same year the public was appalled to read in *The Times* William Howard Russell's revelations of maladministration during the Crimean War. Once more Dickens took up a topical cause and, in his most pessimistic vision of the country, attacked the civil service as the centre of incompetence in a corrupt, prison-like society. His satire in *Little Dorrit* on the 'Circumlocution Office', in which all important business gets stuck, is still one of the finest attacks on bureaucracy we have—a frustrating nightmare vision only excelled by Kafka. Though disputed by many of Dickens's contemporaries, his picture of the exclusive empire of the Barnacle family can be confirmed from contemporary sources, such as a letter of Sir Charles Trevelyan dated 6 February 1854:

There can be no doubt that our high Aristocracy have been accustomed to employ the Civil Establishments as a means of providing for the Waifs and Strays of their Families—as a sort of Foundling Hospital where those who had no energy to make their way in the open professions . . . might receive a nominal office, but real Pension, for life, at the expense of the Public.

Once again it is not factual 'accuracy' alone which matters, but Dickens's re-creation of the experience of meeting with official-dom. Chapter 10 of Book One of *Little Dorrit*—one of the imaginative centres of the novel—follows Arthur Clennam's bewilderment and humiliation as he tries to get information out of the Circumlocution Office, but in vain: after a whole day's effort, Clennam has been referred to 'an airy young Barnacle', who offers him 'plenty of forms to fill up. Lots of 'em here. You can have a dozen if you like.' Still not satisfied, Clennam shocks the young Barnacle with the directness of his next question:

'How shall I find out?'
'Why, you'll—you'll ask till they tell you. Then you'll memorial-ise that Department (according to regular forms which you'll find out) for leave to memorialise this Department. If you get it (which you may after a time), that memorial must be entered in that Department, sent to be registered in this Department, sent back to be signed by that Department, sent back to be counter-signed by this Department and then it will begin to be regularly before that Department. You'll find out when the business passes through each of these stages by asking at both Departments till they tell you.'
'But surely this is not the way to do business,' Arthur Clennam could not help saying.
This airy young Barnacle was quite entertained by his simplicity in supposing for a moment that it was.

(PEL, p157)

So we are introduced to the whole governmental art of 'HOW NOT TO DO IT' (PEL, p145).

By this time Dickens has moved from just attacking specific problems to an integrated vision of a complex world which nothing short of total change can purge of injustice and misery. He continues to revel in his subject, but his humour and vitality are subordinated to a larger end. *Little Dorrit* is as wonderful a novel as *Bleak House*, employing extended imagery to even greater effect. Starting off with a number of scenes of imprisonment and confinement, it proceeds to display the whole world as a prison, from the fraudulent speculator's luxury in Harley Street to the poor community of Bleeding-Heart Yard, through the repressive Calvinist household of Mrs Clennam and the émigré English community in Venice. The Marshalsea Prison in which Mr Dorrit is locked up for years is a microcosm of the outside world and, when Dorrit is suddenly released, it is not to happiness, for he carries the prison with him, in Dickens's most brilliant psychological study of institutionalisation. The final vision of the novel has none of the boisterous hope which attends an early scene of poetic justice, such as the breaking-up of Dotheboys Hall in *Nicholas Nickleby*. Whereas marriage transforms the fictional universe in much comedy, Arthur Clennam and Amy Dorrit are finally married in a world which remains unaltered by their union:

> They went quietly down into the roaring streets, inseparable and blessed; and as they passed along in sunshine and shade, the noisy and the eager, and the arrogant and the froward and the vain, fretted and chafed, and made their usual uproar.
>
> (Book 2, chapter 34, PEL, p895)

Dickens's last completed novel, *Our Mutual Friend* (1864–5), seems to offer hope in the conversion of Bella Wilfer and the moral regeneration of Eugene Wrayburn who marries Lizzie Hexam across a vast social gulf. With its new experiments in narrative forms, its impressive 'set-piece' descriptions, like that in chapter 2 of the Veneerings's dinner-party, and Dickens's most realistic characterisation, including a deep socio-psychological study of Bradley Headstone, the schoolmaster, the book is none the less weakened at the centre by an awkward moral fable of Boffin 'the Golden Dustman' and the corruption of riches. Yet it is the most powerful fictional attack there is on the mid-Victorian bourgeois mentality.

What new realms Dickens was venturing into in the violence and opium visions of his unfinished *The Mystery of Edwin Drood* we can only guess, but his career shows continuous development and experiment right up to his death. His life was one of the most energetic and productive on record, and as a journalist alone he would have a major place in nineteenth-century history. Although certain popular writers had larger audiences than his, he was the most widely read of major English novelists, and while a public figure and social campaigner of great note, he put more of himself and his life into his fiction as transmuted autobiography in books like *David Copperfield* (1849–50) and *Great Expectations*, than any writer apart from James Joyce.

He was on the side of progress, but like most of his radical contemporaries, he feared violence and popular uprising as much as present evils, sounding his alarm in the lovingly described scenes of riot and bloodshed in *Barnaby Rudge* (1841) and *A Tale of Two Cities* (1859). He vividly registered the dominant Victorian ambivalence about change in general, and was simultaneously excited and alarmed, for example, in *Dombey and Son* by the devastation caused as the extension to the London and Birmingham Railway swept away 4,000 houses as it cut its way through to Euston Square in 1838. Like many other Victorians, he felt the impulse to retreat into the past, but he never lost sight of the present. He was one of the heirs of Scott in showing the lives of ordinary people caught up in historical change, and some of his characters, like Scott's, express the everyday courage of ordinary existence. Betty Higden in *Our Mutual Friend* is an example in her proud, independent fear of the workhouse. Dickens could have achieved none of this without his comic genius which transformed his world into something rich and almost bearable, and yet for all that even more deeply disturbing. He touched on so many of the central concerns of his day that Walter Bagehot aptly described him as 'a special correspondent for posterity'.

CHAPTER 8

Industrialisation and the Condition of England

'I too am living by the profit of the factory house. Is this division just?—Oh, God! Is it holy?' cries the wealthy heroine of Frances Trollope's *The Life and Adventures of Michael Armstrong, the Factory Boy* (1840) in her dawning awareness of the misery on which her comfort and prosperity are built. The author explains her heroine's position:

> Mary Brotherton, like perhaps a hundred other rich young ladies, of the same class, grew up in total ignorance of the moans and the misery that lurked beneath the unsightly edifices, which she just knew were called factories, but which were much too ugly in her picturesque eyes for her ever to look at them, when she could help it.

Michael Armstrong is the story of the education of this young lady who, as the conventional novel-reader's representative in the book, is made to discover the living and working conditions of the mill-hands, not at first understanding 'why incessant labour failed to supply the necessaries of life', because like 'multitudes of amiable-minded ladies and gentlemen besides' she believes it 'perfectly impossible such horrors could exist on the glorious soil of Britain'.

Early-Victorian Britain seemed to many people the richest and freest country in the world, but Thomas Carlyle, whose life was devoted to posing embarrassing questions to his fellow-country-men, lashed out at their complacency in *Past and Present* (1843); 'To whom . . . is this wealth of England wealth? Who is it that it blesses; makes happier, wiser, beautifuler, in any way better?' He saw a spiritual and cultural poverty behind the prosperous façade put up by the wealthy, and appalling distress among those whom they exploited:

> Descend where you will into the lower class, in Town or Country, by what avenue you will, by Factory Inquiries, Agricultural Inquiries, by Revenue Returns, by Mining-Labourer Committees, by opening your own eyes and looking, the same sorrowful result discloses itself: you have to admit that the working body of this rich English Nation has sunk or is fast sinking into a state, to which, all sides of it considered, there was literally never any parallel.

It was about this time that English novelists too had begun to probe 'the Condition of England' in documentary fiction, and encouraged by Carlyle's injunction—though he himself had little time for the novel as a literary form—they did descend through statistical reports and personal research into the great social un-known, to examine conditions in the countryside, the new cities of the north, and smaller factory and mining communities.

FRANCES TROLLOPE

Frances Trollope constructed her story in *Michael Armstrong* entirely as a vehicle for descriptions of living and working con-ditions which she had personally investigated in and around the cotton-mills, and in particular isolated prison-like mills, like the Deep Valley Mill in Derbyshire which her heroine visits. Although Mrs Trollope's tale of the lost child, who escapes from the mill and is finally reunited with family and friends, is engaging only during the scenes of adversity and falls flat when it adopts the clichés of sentimental comedy, she none the less reports vividly and compassionately on the things she has seen:

> The ceaseless whirring of a million hissing wheels, seizes on the tortured ear . . . The scents that reek around, from oil, tainted water, and human filth, with that last worst nausea, arising from the hot refuse of atmospheric air, left by some hundred pairs of labouring lungs, render the act of breathing a process of difficulty, disgust, and pain.

The facts themselves are so appalling that it is almost uncharitable to this sturdy pioneer to point out her bad plotting, and her frequent lapses of style, which pass unnoticed for the moment beside the directness of the horrors she presents, for example, in her descriptions of under-sized child-labourers, whose

> [l]ean and distorted limbs—sallow and sunken cheeks—dim hollow eyes, that speak unrest and most unnatural carefulness, give to each tiny, trembling, unelastic form, a look of hideous premature old age.

Having infuriated American public opinion with her brilliantly cutting first book, *The Domestic Manners of the Americans* (1832), and outraged Evangelical readers in Britain with her satirical novel, *The Vicar of Wrexhill* (1837), Mrs Trollope was not one to shy away even from that least known of all strange lands, the industrial north of England. There, writers of the period were forced to act the tourist and explorer, since few of them had detailed or long acquaintance with industrial conditions, except for Elizabeth Gaskell, a Unitarian minister's wife in Manchester. Such a situation contrasts strongly with Dickens's profound grasp of the London scene, in which he thoroughly understood the internal forces and interrelations of the society he described. Novelists investigating the new industrial centres, on the other hand, were faced with quite alien working-class communities whose values they were not equipped to recognise, and whose culture—in the full anthropological sense of the word—they did not understand. Hence, when compared with Dickens's work on the London poor, their fiction always reveals them as outsiders. Pity and charity appear instead of imaginative identification and understanding, and their heartfelt concern cannot help spilling over into condescension, in their well-intentioned attempts to impose alien, middle-class standards on their subjects. Even Dickens was forced to write a quite different type of fiction from his usual in *Hard Times* (1854) when he ventured into the foreign territory of industrial Preston.

This is not to belittle the achievements of novelists like Frances Trollope, Disraeli and Gaskell, who were interpreting the vast floods of official reports and statistics in human terms for their audiences. In this they were performing functions nowadays associated with higher journalism and the social sciences. (Although Engels's *Condition of the Working Class in England* appeared in German in 1845, the English translation was not published until 1887.) In the 1840s the novel had a greater confidence in its own social and political role than ever before or since.

Among other things it set out to examine the moral paradox of industrial capitalism as revealed in de Tocqueville's description of Manchester:

> It is in the midst of this foul drain that the greatest stream of human industry has its source, and goes out to fertilise the whole world. From this filthy sewer flows pure gold. It is here that human nature reaches towards perfection and to brutishness; that civilisation works its miracles, and civilised man reverts almost to a savage.

Novelists' responses to these inbuilt contradictions were as various in their directions as might be expected, but one thing all industrial fiction had in common was the impulse to extend human sympathy into social areas with which literature had not hitherto concerned itself. Wordsworth had already expressed his worry lest violent social change should throw up a new, strange working class beneath whose rags the poet and his reader should be unable to perceive the common humanity, and many novelists of the 1840s were responding—under new circumstances—to the same need to extend their readers' social sympathies, not as Wordsworth did, celebrating the old, disappearing values directly, but squarely confronting the new industrial world.

Like Wordsworth, they were reacting in the main against the power and ideology of the 'millocracy'—'millocrat' is Frances Trollope's word—and, as Wordsworth also did eventually, they often turned to 'safe', familiar, paternalistic Tory ideologies in their fight against the new industrial bourgeoisie. A good case in point is Frances Trollope, whose Toryism goes with a deliberate rejection of the historical alternative, a working-class political movement like Chartism, of which she so strongly disapproved that she could not carry her hero Michael Armstrong on into manhood, because, she explained, Chartist disturbances had made it impossible for her to describe an adult factory-worker sympathetically. Similarly, in *Helen Fleetwood* (1839–41), Charlotte Elizabeth Tonna launched an outraged attack on socialism as 'the *ne plus ultra* of six thousand years' laborious experience on the part of the great enemy of man', while Disraeli for his part wrote some of his novels in order to propagate the idealism of his Young England movement, which aimed explicitly to return to quasi-feudal social relations, as a cure for modern ills.

HARRIET MARTINEAU

One writer very different from these was Harriet Martineau, who espoused the capitalist cause and wrote didactic short stories to propagate the political economy of Ricardo and of James Mill, around whose *Principles of Political Economy* she structured her own *Illustrations of Political Economy* (1832–4). The 1830s, said Bulwer Lytton, were 'the age of political economists . . . Whoever will desire to know hereafter the character of our times, must find it in the philosophy of the Economists.' Martineau was one of the greatest popularisers of the decade, and saw the study of political economy as a 'duty', wishing to persuade her readers to accept the inexorable 'laws' of economics—a resignation not to the will of God but to the economic system. Unlike Adam Smith, she maintained that the interests of master and men were the same, namely—as she states at the end of one of her *Illustrations*—capital accumulation, which alone can ensure the prosperity of all. One of her most famous stories is *A Manchester Strike* (1832), which gives the best description of a strike and of union organisation in Victorian literature, and ends with a set of rules for economic conduct, based on Ricardo's Wages Fund Theory. Perhaps because of her clear partisan position, Martineau saw more about industrial relations and the economic facts of industrial life than her fellow writers of fiction, who concentrated their attention on other more 'human' things, which they recognised as the traditional ingredients of literature. The 1830s were the highpoint of public enthusiasm for political economy, while Dickens's anti-Utilitarian position in *Hard Times* is more typical of feelings in later years, when most writers shared the dislike of Gaskell's heroine in *North and South* (1854-5) of lives organised 'as if commerce were everything and humanity nothing' (chapter 19, OEN, p153).

CHARLOTTE ELIZABETH TONNA

The Evangelical position on the Condition of England was put in *Helen Fleetwood* by 'Charlotte Elizabeth', otherwise Mrs Tonna, who first explored in fiction the experiences of the population forced by need from the country into the cities. The recurrent myth which associates innocence with the country and evil with the town reappears in this novel in a new but emotionally valid way, the country standing for old, familiar social forms with which the contemporary readership could identify. As in Frances Trollope, moral outrage and shocking description carry the reader through a great deal of weak narrative. Conditions in the mill-town finally destroy the heroine and her adoptive family, but while the author is unrestrained in describing her physical horrors, convention forbids her to do more than hint at the moral outrages which are equally to blame for Helen's distress. Blasphemy, Roman Catholicism, Irishness and socialism loom as large in her catalogue of evils as disease and starvation. The tone is unsure, with blatant preaching jarring against realistic description, and a religious style invading the narrative. (It is a bad sign that God 'reigneth' in heaven in the authorial language.) But, like Frances Trollope, Tonna was one of the first to try to alert the public to physical conditions in Britain which were *incomparably more severe*, than any ever produced by negro slavery'.

DISRAELI

The leading polemical writer in the sphere was, of course, Disraeli who used his novels of the 1840s to further the cause of his Young England movement, with which he hoped to revitalise English life and politics by a return to older Tory principles. As fiction his *Coningsby, or the New Generation* (1844) and *Sybil, or the Two Nations* (1845) are vastly superior to Frances Trollope's and Charlotte Tonna's efforts, with fewer static descriptions and far more dramatisation, like the brilliant scenes in the tommy-shop in *Sybil*, which in their vividness eclipse his purely descriptive accounts in the same novel. His range is far wider than Mrs Trollope's or Tonna's, since he aims to examine the state of the whole nation, and systematically refer social conditions to political conditions; but, as regards the new industrial centres, he not surprisingly remains, like his heroes, a 'Gentleman traveller' from the south. When it comes to Westminster and parliamentary politics, on the other hand, this future prime minister is in his element. John Galt's novel *The Member* (1832) was possibly the first fictional account of the procedures and corruptions of Westminster and Whitehall, and of political wheeling and dealing. But Disraeli was aiming higher than Galt's old-fashioned Smollettian satire in wishing to identify the causes of the nation's ills in current party politics and political ideologies, and from historical argument show the youth of the country in this 'age of political infidelity, of mean passions, and petty thoughts' that 'the state of the People' must be cured by the same means as 'the state of the Parties'.

The decline of England, explains Disraeli's all-wise spokesman, Sidonia, stems from 'the fact that the various classes of the country are arrayed against each other'—a state of affairs only to be remedied by a return to older forms of Toryism, with the lead given by young aristocrats who alone have the right and duty to bridge the divide between the Two Nations. Then, Disraeli claims, there would be a return to an England in which Monarchy, Loyalty, Faith and Popular Liberty (all with capital letters) would flourish in a kind of new feudalism. Having rejected Owenite socialism because it puts the community before the family and religion, the young aristocratic paragon, Egremont, in *Sybil*, puts the new Tory case:

> The future principle of English politics will not be a levelling principle; not a principle adverse to privileges, but favourable to their extension. It will seek to ensure equality, not by levelling the Few, but by elevating the Many.
>
> > (*Sybil*, V.ii, 1871 edition, 340)

True social principles derive from 'gentle blood . . . and old English feelings', and changes are to be effected by 'moral power', which the ever-correct Sybil tells us 'is irresistible, or where are we to look for hope?' (p195).

Disraeli embodies his argument in passages of transparently didactic conversation between his perfect young gentlemen and their adversaries and mentors, interspersed among descriptions of the Condition of England and acute satire on existing party politics. The style of these discourses (as befits the political philosophy they expound) is high-flown, stilted and far removed from the everyday, and there is a certain justice in Anthony Trollope's remark that Disraeli's novels have 'a smell of hair-oil, an aspect of buhl, a remembrance of tailors, and that pricking of the conscience which must be the general accompaniment of paste diamonds'. In *Tancred, or the New Crusade* (1847)—which completes a trilogy with *Coningsby* and *Sybil*—it is impossible to take seriously the hero's imitation of his Crusader ancestor in a quest for 'Truth' in the Holy Land, and in its style and gesturings this is surely the silliest novel ever to be taken seriously in English. Perhaps it was the urgency of the Condition of England debate in the 1840s which made considerations of form and design in prose fiction seem otiose; but certainly, like many of his contemporaries, Disraeli did not structure his novels successfully, and was embarrassingly crude in handling his plots. *Sybil*, for example, comes to a quite arbitrary ending in which poetic justice is meted out and happiness constructed for Egremont and Sybil after awkward scenes of violence and melodrama. Yet *Coningsby* and *Sybil* are nevertheless the greatest novels concerning the new industrial society, until Elizabeth Gaskell's.

CHARLES KINGSLEY

Another polemical writer on the Condition of England was Charles Kingsley, whose *Yeast, a Problem* (1848-9 and 1851) presented the fragmented thinking of a generation of university men feeling their way towards a reformation in society, and who went on in *Alton Locke, Tailor and Poet* (1850) to expose conditions in the slums of London, and in the clothing industry in particular. Kingsley was an energetic controversialist, one of the 'Christian Socialists' who campaigned for the spiritual as well as political regeneration of society after the failure of the Chartists' Third National Petition in April 1848. Though opposed to those who advocated physical violence, Kingsley declared himself to be 'a Church of England parson . . . and a Chartist!' and took what was then an extreme democratic stand for one of his class and profession. Christian Socialism now seems far less radical than its enemies feared, for the radical change which it was hoped would sweep the country was meant to avoid popular unrest and leave the existing class structure unchanged, purifying each class instead, by seizing on each individual's heart and soul. The movement was both progressive and reactionary; it believed in science, industry, the dignity of labour and working-class education, yet in wishing for no more (or no less) than a new moral earnestness it sought to reaffirm the established social order.

Yeast reflects this contradiction between radical social criticism and a conservative social blueprint. Kingsley's criticisms of the state of rural England are sharp and well enough directed to be almost revolutionary, yet are set against stilted homilies and conversations on 'manliness' and individual religious conversion, which make the prospect of a just country reformed by a purified aristocracy recede into the regions of the improbable.

The protagonist learns to fulfil himself while moving amongst a schematic cast of representative figures, including the old-fashioned squire, the new industrialist-turned-landowner, the banker, the artist, the noble and virtuous Methodist gamekeeper, the Catholic convert abandoning the world, with woman as purity and inspiration to complete the picture. Both *Yeast* and *Alton Locke* illustrate the Victorian desire for something 'beyond' the actual and everyday in art, in the form of some transcendent ideal. An authorial spokesman in *Yeast* is reported as saying that 'Art was never Art till it was more than Art: that the Finite only existed as the body of the Infinite; and that the man of genius must first know the Infinite, unless he wished to become not a poet, but a maker of idols'. Kingsley preferred to be a smasher of idols, whose aim was a revitalised Church of England as a church for the people, and he angered his fellow-churchmen by describing St Paul's Cathedral during evensong as breathing 'imbecility, and unreality, and sleepy life-in-death, while the whole nineteenth century went roaring on its way outside'. Kingsley was a campaigner who turned to the novel for definite purposes and who cared little enough for fictional design summarily to kill off his heroine in *Yeast* at the behest of the editor of the magazine in which it was appearing, when the circulation seemed to be falling.

ELIZABETH GASKELL

Elizabeth Gaskell, on the other hand, was a novelist with urgent things to say, but so much more the novelist in her impulse and skills that a coherent vision of life emerges from her writings and not a series of observations with moral lessons attached. Her earliest novel, *Mary Barton, a Tale of Manchester Life* (1848) was the first Condition of England novel in which the author imaginatively identified with her working-class characters. Around 1840 what most occupied C. E. Tonna, Frances Trollope and other writers and philanthropists was the appalling plight of child-labourers, but by 1848—'the year of revolutions' abroad and of riots and agitation in Britain—the suffering and unrest of 'the hungry forties' had pushed the general causes of proletarian discontent into prominence as the leading concern of the age.

Gaskell wrote about the same Manchester which Engels had unforgettably described a few years before in *The Condition of the Working Class in England*. Unlike Tonna and Trollope, she did not restrict herself to external descriptions of industrial horrors, although the desperate want, the inhumanity and the injustice were more closely felt here than in any other fiction. Her strength lay in presenting a rounded view of her characters' life—a plausible human and social existence, complete with its joys and relaxations as well as its sufferings—so that she not only avoided condescending pity but revealed the full strengths and resources of the Manchester working class. While some writers presented an image of a proletariat so abject, almost bestial, that its protests could only issue in inchoate growls or drunken disorder, Gaskell pointed to the thoughtful, educated members of the class who historically were the strength in the growing labour movement. *Mary Barton* shows the struggles and the dignity of industrial life by an identification with characters who have a full psychological existence and speak about their own lives in credible, moving but unsentimental voices, like that of Alice relating how she moved from the country in her youth. Their language is proved to be an adequate vehicle for their experience and is not treated as a 'lower' comic or pathetic style. If need be, the middle-class reader is helped by means of footnotes, but the spoken language is not debased.

When, in the first part of *Mary Barton*, Gaskell dramatises the contrast between the misery of the workers and the wealth of the employers, she is noticing things which no comfortable, received middle-class opinions can explain away,. but like her fellow-writers she eventually assumes the need for a reconciliation between the classes. On the way her desire for a plot has led her to transform her Tale of Manchester Life into a rather melodramatic story of murder and revenge, which concludes with a symbolic repentance scarcely relevant to the social vision of the opening. But her success is seen by comparing hers with Charlotte Brontë's handling of workers in *Shirley* (1849), where deep development of the middle-class protagonists' individual conflicts and frustrations prohibits more than an external treatment of their class enemy, and this very interesting attempt at combining personal and social problems in one story falters through a thin presentation of the public events.

Gaskell's greatest novel, *North and South*, is successful exactly in this respect, in combining the private and the social in one story by exploiting both the scope of the social novel and the method of minute analysis bequeathed by Jane Austen. Like Frances Trollope in *Michael Armstrong* and Charlotte Brontë in *Shirley*, Gaskell exposes a heroine to disturbing new experiences and does it by transporting a clergyman's family from the New Forest in the rural south to a great industrial city, Milton, in the north. At first a naïve contrast seems set up between the paternalistic south, full of sunny charm and the traditional values of English culture, and the struggling, brutal north, an 'unhealthy, smoky, sunless place', whose ungenteel values are work and profit. By introducing a conscientious mill-owner in the person of Mr Thornton, Gaskell gets beyond Frances Trollope's unuseful picture of individually wicked millocrats, each personally to blame for the system; Thornton puts across quite vigorously various things she herself does not believe—such as the reality of a class struggle which writers as antithetical as Martineau and Dickens tried to ignore by positing the 'identity of interest' between masters and men, and which Gaskell's clergyman mystifies in broad Christian terms as the need to work for 'the good of all, instead of that of merely one class as opposed to another' (chapter 28, OEN, p233). As Margaret Hale's understanding of the Milton way-of-life progresses (the narrative language gradually taking on Lancashire forms in the process, by the way) her, and her author's, ambivalent attitude towards industrial activity deepens. Here is a description of Milton just before Thornton's bankruptcy:

> ... the chimneys smoked, the ceaseless roar and mighty beat, and dizzying whirl of machinery, struggled and strove perpetually. Senseless and purposeless were wood and iron and steam in their endless labours; but the persistence of their monotonous work was rivalled in tireless endurance by the strong crowds, who, with sense and with purpose, were busy and restless ...
>
> (chapter 50, OEN, p418)

The complex of attitudes is complete when the heroine returns to her old home, only to find it a place of change and of such cruelty and superstition that even the 'soft green influence [of the woods] could not charm away the shock and the pain in Margaret's heart' and she becomes perforce reconciled to certain paradoxes of existence and to the reality of progress (chapter 46, OEN, p390).

The only industrial solutions Gaskell can envisage are human contact between employers and workmen, and a watered-down version of Owenite communal living. As in *Mary Barton*, Gaskell's dramatisation is vastly superior to her analysis, but the humanity of these two industrial novels is not all that guarantees her fame, for her six novels taken together display that broad, generous scope in their treatment of individuals and society which is frequently characterised as typically Victorian.

Dickens was a writer of even greater range, but his one industrial novel, *Hard Times*, is not easily appreciated in the context of his other major works, nor does it resemble any other industrial novel of the time. He incorporated nothing in the way of realistic description of what he had seen during his visit to Preston in January 1854, when he had written back to his friend John Forster in London, 'I am afraid I shall not be able to get much here . . . there is very little in the streets to make the town remarkable.' A comparison of *Hard Times* with his straightforward reporting in an article 'On Strike' in *Household Words* of 11 February 1854 shows that his aim was not documentary fiction but a fabular world rather like those of *An Old Curiosity Shop* or *The Christmas Books*; for even in his most insistently symbolic novels, like *Little Dorrit* or *Our Mutual Friend*, his fable is usually made concrete by a wealth of developed detail about the characters' domestic and working lives. Faced with the industrial north where he knew little of home or factory life, he presented instead a brilliant satirical and sentimental vision of a clash of Utilitarian ideology with common warmth and humanity. His satire on the Utilitarian educationalists in the person of Mr M'Choakumchild is among his sharpest, and his attack on those who smugly appealed to Samuel Smiles's principle of Self-Help cuts deeply at a dominant social orthodoxy:

> Any capitalist there, who had made sixty thousand pounds out of sixpence, always professed to wonder why the sixty thousand nearest Hands didn't each make sixty thousand pounds out of sixpence, and more or less reproached them every one for not accomplishing this little feat.
>
> (II.i, PEL, p152)

On the other hand, he is misleading on industrial life. His protagonist, Stephen Blackpool, is obtuse to the point of stupidity, and so unusual among the workers that his case is unrevealing; his misery stems as much from his marriage to an alcoholic as from the industrial situation, he refuses on principle to join a union and he certainly does not represent the thinking of his class in understanding no more about the world than that it is 'aw a muddle'. Despite its successes, the weakness of *Hard Times* is that while it effectively attacks the millocracy's political economy, it illogically comes round to a belief, like Harriet Martineau's, in co-operation between mill-owners and workers, which in Dickens's view can only be effective through a general pleasant-ness and change of heart in those concerned. It is not that Sleary's circus is an inadequate symbol of human warmth and freedom, but that it is given too much to do in the novel, where it must serve to conceal the inconsistencies in Dickens's position.

The myth of identity of interest stems from a general alarm at class conflict—a fear principally of disorder, and by extension of any mass movement—and a yearning, like Carlyle's or Kingsley's, for a stable social order. During the 1840s and even later, too, when the danger of revolution had receded, a fear of violence haunted the middle class, and emotions appropriate to Chartist riots were somewhat melodramatically transferred wholesale on to trades unions, reinforced by memories of secret societies with blood-thirsty oaths (like the one Dandy Mick swears in *Sybil*), and the image of the '[s]trange faces of pale men, with dark glaring eyes' in *Mary Barton*, or threatening messages poignarded to non-union workers' doors in Reade's *Put Yourself in His Place* (1870).

In less melodramatic contexts, too, most Victorian writers dis-approved of trades unions for putting group objectives before individual desires and duties, and as the Victorian novel was particularly adapted to the examination of individual moral cases there was a limit to its analysis of the problems of a whole class, not having for the contemporary scene the facility for which Scott was famed of representing a complete section of society through a typical spokesman. For Dickens, unions coerced the individual worker and were therefore bad, while for George Eliot class solidarity and mass action required an impermissible simplifi-cation and vulgarisation of moral judgement. So, in *Felix Holt the Radical* (1866), her presentation of the moral case of a landed character like Mrs Transome is satisfying and complete in every detail, and her analysis of Felix's own feelings in resisting union activities is perfectly consistent, but it is not within her normal scope—broad though that is—fully to understand the union cause.

Despite its whole polemical variety and excitement, the Condition of England fiction of the 1840s and 1850s reveals all the time that the novel had largely been developed to register bourgeois consciousness and, whatever other successes it might score, it would always most easily deal with the middle-class individual in the bourgeois world.

CHAPTER 9

Victorian Views of the Individual

The Brontes, Thackeray, Trollope and George Eliot

THE BRONTËS

Without question the most confident celebration of the individual's will and passions in English fiction is Emily Brontë's *Wuthering Heights*, a novel whose action is deliberately set far away from the populous haunts of men, and in which such social conventions, duties and restraints as are allowed room appear only in order to be swept away in a tempest of uncurbed emotion. In this, the novel is exceptional in Victorian fiction, where one of the principal concerns is usually the relationship—complex or strained though it may be—of the individual with his or her society. Charlotte Brontë's protagonists, for example, eventually find a place of some sort for themselves in the world, despite a threatening environment, while one of the greatest achievements of mid-Victorian novelists was to display and evaluate the individual's conduct against a working fictional society, and show his strengths and weaknesses by how he succumbed to or negotiated his environment.

Wuthering Heights is quite uncompromising in following the fullest development of the passions and impulses of the romantic individual, but despite the overthrow of—or, rather, the total disregard for—conventional morality, the novel is not in any acceptable sense of the word immoral; the principal characters and events are presented as being outside the confines of commonplace moral standards. So extraordinary indeed are the speech, motives and actions of the protagonists that the reader has to be buffered from them by the device of a narrative-within-a-narrative, so that the alien material is filtered through the general narrator, Mr Lockwood—rather ordinary and mundane as he is—who witnesses Heathcliff in his later years, and the two informative servants: Nelly Dean, humane, anxious and limited in her way, and Joseph, uncouth, superstitious and limited in his, who expresses himself in a carefully rendered but very thick dialect. The story of love, betrayal, death and revenge emerging through these carefully arranged indirections, through flashbacks and time-gaps, is one which to the commonplace mind of Lockwood (and the reader) throws confusion on established moral categories. But, rather than simply linking opposites in a dark, fatalistic vision of existence—as Byron arguably does with his ambivalent heroes—Emily Brontë astonishingly leaves the usual Christian concepts of good and evil on one side.

In this extreme romantic assertion of the power of the exceptional character, everyday categories are ignored in a tempest of emotion. Love is not a mere feeling or inclination but a fundamental, irreversible identification—a question indeed of personal identity and existence—and all this is refracted through two layers of imperfectly comprehending narrative report by witnesses left bemused by violent outbursts whose intensity they cannot share, like Cathy's 'Nelly, I *am* Heathcliff!' (chapter 9, PEL, p122). Love is finally and, in the terms of the novel, logically consummated by union after death, when—the reader is almost convinced he should believe—the ghosts of Cathy and Heathcliff walk their beloved moors, as Joseph reports they do.

The wildness of the setting on the Yorkshire moors which featured so large in Emily Brontë's experience, the strangeness of the psychological events and the intensity of the imagery of fire, storm and demonism surrounding the characters make *Wuthering Heights* unique in English prose. Yet the patterns are all psychoanalytically recognisable, as though Emily Brontë had an exceptionally clear channel of communication with the subconscious. The psychologically threatening material is encompassed and made just safe enough in a most carefully structured narrative form, which owes much and serves a purpose similar to that of the more extravagant gothic and romantic novels of a few decades earlier. Only Hogg's *Memoirs and Confessions of a Justified Sinner* can be compared in terms of its success in controlling and making credible the most extraordinary material without devaluing it.

It is tempting to overemphasise the connexions between the works of the three Brontë sisters, when they had in fact highly individual styles and preoccupations. Yet the closeness of their family ties, the unparalleled burst of family creativity which produced seven novels, six of them within three years, and the fact of their living and writing outside the London literary world and the ambit of the publishing houses inevitably separate them somewhat from other novelists of the 1840s and 1850s.

Although Charlotte shared something of Emily's intensity, her unusually explicit recognition of female sexuality and her powerful use of imagery, such as fire and storm, in projecting strong emotions and a dangerous environment, the forms and concerns of her four novels are quite different. Instead of presenting characters as the unimpeded flowering of individual, simple, passionate essences, Charlotte sees human life as a long struggle for existence between the individual and her or his environment, after which a reconciliation may perhaps be achieved, but at some personal cost. *Jane Eyre* (1847) and *Villette* (1852) are each first-person accounts of their heroine's lives, but at the end of the novel it is not so much that the narrator has learnt the lessons of the world and can now fit into some comfortable berth in society —as can Gil Blas or one of Smollett's heroes—as that she has endured an antagonistic social environment until such time as a compromise could be reached. Together with the earlier *The Professor* (written in 1846 but published in 1856) these are investigations of the self-sufficiency and strategies of survival necessary to preserve the protagonist in the world, and find a middle way between the repression of passion and surrender to it. At this level of analysis, nothing could less resemble Emily's fiction.

Jane Eyre is the story of an orphan who as a child resists both the cruelty and the dehumanising charity of those around her, and as she grows up can only maintain her inner, secret freedom, by self-abnegation and the humiliating social dependence of being a governess. She repels her employer's bigamous proposal, but after his mad, concealed wife has set fire to the house and perished in the flames, Jane accepts him, blind, maimed and chastened—a wounded eagle. Charlotte Brontë used a great deal of autobiographical material, but it is unprofitable to take Jane's story as her creator's, even at a purely psychological level. *Villette*, too, incorporates an abundance of the novelist's own experience and observation, but the heroine, Lucy Snowe—who is partially characterised in her name—is a very different character from Jane. Like Jane though, she is a social outsider and nurses a precious secret self within her, which she feels she must preserve intact in the face of a hostile world where she is forced to play roles at variance with the innermost core of her personality; but, unlike Jane, she is not immediately appealing to the reader, and the novelist's whole skill must be used to generate sympathy for her.

The fictional worlds of these novels are completely centred on their narrators, with all other characters presented only in so far as they impinge on them, the narrators never desiring to undertake any disinterested inquiry into traits and circumstances which do not immediately affect them. Despite the careful social observation of things like a governess's predicament in an upper-class drawing-room in *Jane Eyre*, character typology does not follow a social scheme but is based entirely on characters' roles as sympathisers, or as social or erotic threats to the heroine. So Charlotte Brontë's novels centre on the individual strenuously coping with the world and, although the protagonist is not triumphant in any heroic sense, it is the individual who is supremely important throughout, even in *Shirley*, where the novelist worked at a more substantial, more extended social environment than elsewhere. There is no outright heroism in these novels, but considerations of the individual rule their fictional worlds.

THACKERAY

The English novel rarely had time for the heroic. A Fielding or a Smollett protagonist was meant to be, in Samuel Johnson's phrase, 'levelled with the rest of mankind', while Scott's central characters were not usually interesting by reason of their sensitivity or ability but from the circumstances in which they were placed. Thackeray would seem to have been obeying a trend in English fiction in entitling his first novel *Vanity Fair, a Novel without a Hero* (1847–8), holding as he did 'that the Art of Novels is . . . to convey as strongly as possible the sentiment of reality as opposed to a tragedy or poem, which may be heroical'. But the implications of his title are more radical than this, for the satirical vision of *Vanity Fair* does not admit any of the qualities necessary to heroic status. Human conduct is ruled by large and small vices, not virtues, and the appearance of virtue is normally construed as a mask for vice. Great men are great by virtue of their positions and their trappings, for, as Thackeray delights to quote, 'no man is a hero to his valet', and his caricatures of Louis XIV dressed and undressed show the splendid Sun King as a combination of gorgeous robes and a feeble, shrivelled old man. But for Thackeray the satiric lash is not wielded from a high position of moral superiority. The satirist himself is part of universally erring mankind, prematurely aged and world-weary with the recognition of life's deficiencies.

When he wrote *Vanity Fair* he already had behind him years of experience of shorter fiction, satire and burlesque on *Fraser's Magazine* and *Punch*; this first novel shows a more consistent satirical approach than his later ones and, with its deliberate patterning of characters, a more secure sense of design than any except *The History of Henry Esmond* (1852). Of the two female protagonists in *Vanity Fair*, a novel with neither heroes nor heroines, Becky Sharp is delightfully wicked and appealing, and frequently passes truly disturbing reflections on social mores by asserting, for example, that she could be a virtuous woman on £5,000 a year. Amelia Sedley, on the other hand, is bloodlessly virtuous to a fault and is eventually judged accordingly by the authorial voice, for all its previous expressions of sentimental attachment to her. Such ambivalences are the key to Thackeray. What his contemporaries read as the cynicism of his satire is not necessarily antithetical to his sentiment, since the objects of the satire are often attractive, if only in their vitality or resilience, and their vices are common both to the author and—as he is careful to point out—to his readers as well. His sentiment is never straightforward for long. Dobbin is clearly judged to be foolish in devoting himself to Amelia, while Colonel Newcome in *The Newcomes* (1853–5), for all his paternal virtues, is a major problem in Clive's life and an obstacle to his artistic development. Just as a sentimental cliché seems to have been established, Thackeray will turn it suddenly sour with a new slant on the subject. In *Pendennis* (1848–50) he expands for a while on the sentimental Victorian commonplace of man as 'the oak (or the post)' and woman as 'the ivy or the honeysuckle whose arms twine about him', only to undercut it with the vision of the Arcadian lover, Damon, standing 'like a British man with his hand in his breeches pocket, while the pretty fond parasite clings round him' (chapter 56).

It is not Thackeray's way to examine the causes of these distorting sex-stereotypes in society. What he does is to disturb conventional notions, while registering at the same time with humorous bitterness many forms of male fear of women, in passive as much as in aggressive roles, and he rudely touches on forbidden matters when he looks at a woman's pain at finding herself 'mated for life to a boor, and ordered to love and honour a dullard', and the dull man's corresponding alarm

> that his slave and drudge yonder is, in truth, his superior . . . that she can think a thousand things beyond the power of his muddled brain; and that in yonder head, on the pillow opposite to him, lie a thousand feelings, mysteries of thought, latent scorns and rebellions, whereof he only dimly perceives the existence . . .
>
> (*Esmond*, I.xi)

Thackeray is particularly good at recording the desolating loneliness implicit in a certain kind of individualist view of the world, in which nobody can have any knowledge of other minds, and everyone has distressing, shameful or nonsensical thoughts to conceal. In a famous passage in *Pendennis*, he expatiates on this in his conversational, 'essay' style, firmly implicating himself and his public in what he is saying:

> Thus, oh friendly readers, we see every man in the world has his own private griefs and business, by which he is more cast down or occupied than by the affairs or sorrows of any other person . . . How lonely we are in the world! how selfish and secret, everybody! You and your wife have pressed the same pillow for forty years and fancy yourselves united.—Psha, does she cry out when you have the gout, or do you lie awake when she has the tooth-ache? . . . Ah, sir—a distinct universe walks about under your hat and under mine—all things in nature are different to each—the woman we look at has not the same features, the dish we eat from has not the same taste to the one and the other—you and I are but a pair of infinite isolations, with some fellow-islands a little more or less near to us.
>
> (chapter 16)

As a satirist in an age profoundly distrustful of satire, Thackeray's position was difficult. He was perpetually accused of cynicism and was perhaps alarmed himself at the reductionist tendency in his moral vision, feeling it implied the possibility that, if the pomp and deception were stripped from the world, there might be nothing left at all—hence his use of the 'language of the heart', and his appeal to the 'eternal' qualities of human nature which supposedly represented a 'truth' to stand against the flux of time. In terms of his satirical vision, this is rather soft, wishful thinking; but his is not a fully unified vision of life, and the tensions are essential to the dynamic and sparkle of his fiction. The contradictions of life remain unresolved, and are preserved in the saddened experience and memory of the authorial persona.

This is self-conscious art, somewhat like Fielding's, which constantly reveals itself as art and claims for itself a higher importance as a comment on life than any fiction that masquerades as fact. Thackeray's authorial stance in this respect gave him as much trouble with his readers as his unflattering view of human nature, for in general the Victorian public preferred a type of novel which did not appear to distinguish between real life and make-believe. A novel, it was widely felt, should be totally transparent, and its 'content' in terms of characters and events should be revealed unclouded by any evidence of formal and stylistic contrivance on the author's part. It is not possible to exert sufficient self-deception to ignore Thackeray's controlling hand; he not only comments in his fiction on the course of his story but openly admits that he manipulates his creatures like puppets, or that they exist in some 'Fable-land' of the imagination, in which things may be settled for the best. For him, art is a consolation, and also imposes a certain arbitrary order on existence, to rescue something out of the dubious flux of experience. Yet, sensing a danger of total moral relativism if his framework were purely aesthetic, Thackeray takes refuge in a rather sickly religiosity—just as he does in his account of human nature—and ties his aestheticism to a quasi-religious idealism: 'Art is truth: and truth is religion; and its study and practice a daily work of pious duty' (*Newcomes*, chapter 64).

Among other things, Thackeray's novels render the mixture of sense-impressions jostling with memories in the consciousness and, as the fiction is admittedly in the memory or imagination of the authorial persona, he is free to move back and forth chronologically at will. For example, when Miss Bunion is related to have 'set down' Pendennis 'as a prig', the narrative can suddenly slip forward some years into a later conversation, with 'She told him so much in after days with her usual candour', so that a new light is cast on the significance of the earlier events (chapter 34). When Clive Newcome sees Ethel again in later years, he perceives her for a while at two different moments in time simultaneously:

> And the past and its dear histories, and youth and its hopes and passions, and tones and looks for ever echoing in the heart, and present in the memory—these, no doubt, poor Clive saw and heard as he looked across the great gulf of time, and parting and grief, and beheld the woman he had loved for many years. There she sits; the same, but changed; as gone from him as if she were dead; departed indeed into another sphere . . .
>
> (chapter 66)

In a fragmented way, Thackeray had many of the perceptions about time which Marcel Proust was to make the subject of his great novel *Remembrance of Things Past* (1912–27) and, like Proust, Thackeray sometimes rounds off his fiction with a fictionalised account of its composition, so that to an important degree it is about itself. In Proust, such ideas as Thackeray touches on from time to time are united into a large scheme in which memory is the guarantee of identity through time, and literature a kind of magical custodian of memory. Across the years—'echoing in the heart', in Thackeray's phrase—the older Marcel has heard his parents' garden bell in Combray and resolves, in his search for time lost to the past, to write the very novel the reader is just finishing:

> When [the bell] rang I already existed, and since then, in order that I should continue to hear this ringing, there could necessarily have been no discontinuity, and I could not for a moment have ceased to exist, to think, to be conscious of myself, because that

former moment clung to me, and I could still return to it, merely by plunging more deeply into myself . . . I felt dizzy at seeing so many years beneath me, or rather, within me, as if I were leagues high . . . At least if [the strength of my memory] were left to me for long enough to accomplish my work, I should not fail to describe men (though it should make them resemble monstrous beings) as occupying a most considerable place in time, beside the so restricted one which is reserved for them in space, a place on the contrary, immeasurably prolonged—since like giants immersed in the years, they touch simultaneously on widely separated periods, between which so many days have come and ranged them selves—in Time.

Thackeray, who wrote too often without a sufficient plan and improvised his story from month to month, could not have developed an adequate form to exploit *his* vision to the full, and consequently his elucidation of his protagonists' consciousness is a trifle commonplace beside Proust's.

Form was a perpetual problem to Thackeray. Despite a strong admiration for Fielding, he had none of Fielding's mastery of plot as significant form, and was apparently casual on questions of structure and consistency of tone in all his novels except *Vanity Fair* and *Esmond*. He was unusual in his age in openly preferring the previous century to his own, finding the frankness of Hogarth and the eighteenth-century novelists a relief from Victorian moral squeamishness. He lovingly set both the action and the language of *Esmond* in the reign of Queen Anne, with *The Virginians* (1857–9) following later in the century, and *Vanity Fair* in the last period of fashionable glitter in his own century, the Regency world. He may perhaps have displayed a considerable neurosis in furthering the ends of the dull respectability he disliked, yet encouraged, with his notions of middle-class gentility and the purity of women; but he represented a puzzle to his contemporaries in openly championing eighteenth-century cultural standards. He was a successful writer, but wrote principally for men of his own class, around the London clubs. A liking for Thackeray was an educated taste, but the intelligentsia of subsequent generations scorned his sentiment and his reputation suffered accordingly. In the middle years of the century, however, his name and that of Dickens dominated the world of the novel.

With *Vanity Fair*, *Pendennis*, *The Newcomes* and *The Virginians*, Thackeray had followed Dickens's highly successful method of publication in separate monthly parts, but from 1860 he took a principal role in a new kind of publishing venture as editor of the *Cornhill Magazine*, the most successful of the many cheap middle-class monthlies established around that date to purvey serial fiction and offer not only novels by Thackeray, Trollope and George Eliot but serious articles by leading authorities on the arts, science, philosophy and current affairs.

ANTHONY TROLLOPE

The *Cornhill* was launched in 1860 with a new novel by Anthony Trollope, *Framley Parsonage*, his ninth, and the fourth to deal with his fictional county of Barsetshire. It and the magazine in which it appeared were an immediate success, selling 100,000 copies per month, and Trollope became firmly established for the best part of the decade as the leading interpreter of the lives of the landed and professional classes of the time.

In a certain respect Trollope followed Thackeray, whose aim was to examine moral conduct in such a way that a term like 'gentleman' might lose its class exclusivity and embrace the qualities of uprightness and responsibility in which the middle classes prided themselves, and to investigate what one critic called 'the debatable land between the middle classes and the aristocracy'. In periods of considerable class mobility, literature had often not only castigated 'vulgar' pretension but also actively advised newly prosperous social groups on matters of conduct; it is worth viewing Trollope's role as a social mentor in the light of a comment by Johnson in his *Life of Addison*, when he points out what bourgeois literature lacked before the *Spectator* appeared on the scene at the beginning of the eighteenth century:

We had many books to teach us our more important duties, and to settle opinions in philosophy or politics; but an *Arbiter Elegantiarum*, a judge of propriety, was yet wanting, who should survey the track of daily conversation, and free it from thorns and prickles, which teaze the passer, though they do not wound him.

As a novelist beloved of the middle-class circulating libraries, Trollope did exactly that for his primary public of members of his own professional class, who would not have regarded this as an unimportant service in an age when it was a commonplace to look to the middle class 'for the safety of England', and it could be uncontroversially asserted that 'the professional classes . . . form the head of the great English middle class, maintain its tone of independence, keep up to the mark its standard of morality, and direct its intelligence'. Writing, as he himself indicated, for his fellow clubmen, civil servants, lawyers, politicians and clergymen, Trollope captivated this class by projecting an unparalleled picture of their everyday lives, so that it was said that to the future historian his novels 'will picture the society of our day with a fidelity with which society has never been pictured before in the history of the world'.

His fiction, however, is more interesting than the unselfconscious approbation of some of these contemporaries might suggest. He was deeply interested in individual moral choice in relation to the increasing pressures of the modern environment, in an age which Tennyson had announced as one in which '. . . the individual withers, and the world is more and more' ('Locksley Hall' 1837, l.142). As one critic wrote in 1859, 'The individual's struggle with society is [Trollope's] theme, the characteristics which secure success and failure his study', while another conceded that '[n]o one grasps more strongly the difference between a man who floats with the tide and a man who is pushing his way upwards to a higher moral faith'. The struggle involved a person's duty to his sense of self, his family and friends, and his station in life, and—in the interaction of these factors—his social and personal identity.

Most of Trollope's major characters spend a great deal of time considering the rights and wrongs of their own past or future actions—searching their consciences but responding to social, conventional moral standards, and not to eternal religious truths, for neither Trollope's mind nor his fiction are religious and it is a kind of secular conscience that interests him. Victorian religious doubt involved taking a new look at the conscience. Religious thinkers and philosophical idealists considered human character to be innate, and the conscience to be that part of the given that governed moral judgements, in terms of *a priori* ethical knowledge, and Jeremiah could be quoted to show as much: 'After those days, said the Lord, I will put my law in their inward part and write it in their hearts' (xxxi, 33). Religious sceptics had to find an adequate non-metaphysical explanation for a sense of right and wrong, since a sceptical system which did not provide a satisfactory account of the conscience stood little chance of success—and, besides, all Victorian thinkers recognised an internal moral voice in themselves. Leslie Stephen illustrates the agnostic position perfectly when he writes in a letter of 1865, 'I now believe in nothing, to put it shortly; but do not the less believe in morality, &c. &c. I mean to live and die like a gentleman if possible.' Like George Eliot, Stephen appeals to humanistic standards instead of religious authority; personal and social morality will not be affected, but the rationale behind them must be revised.

Trollope's characters possess just this kind of secular conscience, so that the questions with which he seems almost obsessed in his fiction—such as what it means to be a gentleman, and whether a certain person is behaving in a manner becoming to a gentleman—are not a matter of mere social scruple but are basic to a whole complex of mid-Victorian morality. What appear at first sight to be questions of manners turn out, in the context of an age disturbed by the increasing secularisation of its thought, to be vital moral issues. Such questions inevitably involve considerations of social status, too, in a society where individual morality was universally held to be the basis of social health, and was to be inculcated in the masses by the teaching and example of their 'betters'.

Trollope's view of human character ran him foul of his religious and idealist critics, because he showed no *a priori* essence of character as a basis for personality, and because his characters examine their secular consciences in terms of their experience and action in the world around them rather than in relation to any eternal verities or transcendental ideas. As the novelist of the social life of the Church of England, Trollope hardly shows himself interested in spiritual exercise at all and, since he regarded Cicero as a model for what a Christian gentleman should be, it is clear that his conception of Christianity was purely humanistic; although, like many of his contemporaries, he fell back on a cautious doctrine of spiritual utility, whereby it was supposed to be to the general good that the mass of the population should believe in some religion which would keep them under effective moral control.

Like some important thinkers of his period, Trollope seems to have held environmentalist views of the conscience and thought of moral sense as built up within the mind of the individual on the model of the laws operating in the world outside. Nevertheless he has little or no interest in developmental psychology, and what concerns him is the dilemma of an adult—young or old—trying to reconcile his sense of self with the demands of conscience and his position in society. 'There is nothing in the world so difficult as that task of making up one's mind', the authorial voice tells us in *Phineas Finn, the Irish Member* (chapter 60, PEL, p573). The hero of this novel feels he must vote against his party on the matter of Irish tenant-right as a question of conscience and because he is Irish himself; but meanwhile he knows that, if he does so, he must resign his minor government position at a time when he is in debt yet sees a bright political future ahead. In *Can You Forgive Her?*

Alice Vavasour wishes she could enter politics, but does not want (nor does Trollope) the public and domestic revolution which would be necessary before women would be allowed into Parliament; so she must make her marriage choice not only on the grounds of love or liking but with reference to how largely she could participate in politics through a husband and his position. In *The Claverings* Harry Clavering has been jilted by his cousin, Julia, in favour of a dissolute nobleman, Lord Ongar. Harry is from a landed family but obliged to earn his living and, although a fellow of his Cambridge college, is working as a schoolmaster. His sense of identity is closely tied up with these equivocal parameters of social status, and he is equally hurt by Julia's inconstancy, her rise in society and her taunts at his slightly demeaning occupation. He later becomes an engineer, joining a new profession which has not yet been granted social respectability.

Profession is of key importance. The three protagonists of *The Three Clerks* (1858) respond in different ways to their civil service jobs, with every nuance of status carefully played up and every temptation to personal and professional corruption explored to the full. Alaric Tudor, from the high-status Weights and Measures Office, is finally imprisoned for corruption, while Charley Tudor, in the lowly Internal Navigation Office, manages to save himself from a dreadful social precipice when he just does not marry a barmaid. These cases, and the problems of Lady Mason, in *Orley Farm* (1861–2), who once forged a codicil to her late husband's will, are only a few examples of the total interdependence of character and society which makes Trollope fascinating reading for modern clinical psychologists.

Each Trollopian individual is trapped in his or her own head in the midst of a crowded, jostling world, which the author renders with generous scope in the course of his many long novels. However lengthy by today's standards, the Victorian three-volume novel was essential to the gradual build-up of an extensive fictional world, but Trollope went outside even these bounds, and linked six novels together at a time, in a depiction of middle- and upper-class life which was as broad in time as it was in geography and the size of its cast. His first famous novel, *The Warden* (1855), dealt with a case of conscience concerning the administration of a charitable trust in the fictional cathedral city of Barchester; from there he first of all expanded his vision to the church affairs of all Barchester in *Barchester Towers* (1857), and thence embraced the dealings of the clergy and the landed and professional classes of the whole county of Barsetshire, to end in one of his intensest psychological studies in *The Last Chronicle of Barset* (1866–7). Overlapping with this rather fortuitous sequence came another, more important series of novels, centring on the marriage and political career of Plantagenet Palliser and his wife, Lady Glencora, who had been joined in a frigid, arranged match in one of the Barsetshire novels. Everyone knew that the six *Chronicles of Barsetshire* were linked, but with his popularity declining from 1870 onwards Trollope doubted whether anybody would recognise the far more ambitious continuity between *Can You Forgive Her?* (1864–5), *Phineas Finn* (1867–9), *The Eustace Diamonds* (1871–3), *Phineas Redux* (1873–4), *The Prime Minister* (1875–6) and *The Duke's Children* (1879–80)—on which rests his modern reputation as a major novelist.

He was not the first novelist to re-utilise characters from previous books in creating a large vision of the world; Thackeray had done it before him—rather archly and sentimentally—but so, more importantly, had Balzac in his vast panorama of French Restoration society, *La comédie humaine* (1831–47). Trollope worked by developing a multiplicity of individuals and bringing them into repeated and varied contact with each other, while Balzac proceeded more intellectually from quasi-scientific 'laws' of society, with a deliberation which makes Trollope appear somewhat amateurish. Both Balzac and Trollope had divided sympathies for the different sectors of the societies they were describing, and are in this way particularly valuable registers of the social movements of their periods. Balzac without question preferred the aristocracy to the rising bourgeoisie, yet admired the energy of those who were changing society, reserving some of his sharpest scorn for reactionary lassitude; while Trollope celebrated the struggle for power of his own upper-middle class, and yet in much of his fiction seems emotionally to have identified with the old Tory squirearchy.

Trollope's successes are great. A large and consistent picture of mid-Victorian England emerges from his work, his description of social behaviour and manners is definitive, his dialogue and dramatic scenes are direct and amusing, and when, as it frequently is, the authorial voice is heard, it is as often as not giving brief comments or longer disquisitions on the rules governing the world of the novels—acting, that is, as a social analyst at a high level. His extended social studies are central to an understanding of mid-Victorian fiction in general. Other writers, great and small, aimed at similar effects, and it is not far-fetched to say that, if we fail to appreciate his successes, we do not notice some of the fundamental qualities of even greater fiction like George Eliot's *Middlemarch*.

GEORGE ELIOT

Trollope concentrated on the dilemmas of individual moral choice within a largely social context, while George Eliot investigated somewhat similar problems from the carefully worked-out position of a religious humanist. Her first fiction, *Scenes of Clerical Life*, was published in 1857, the same year as the second of Trollope's Barsetshire novels; but, though they both deal with the clergy, their subjects are completely different. George Eliot does not take the social and political life of the Church of England as her theme; having abandoned the evangelical religion in which she was brought up, she uses religious life as a kind of metaphor for moral life, in a scheme of things which rejects orthodox Christianity but retains its moral lessons, and seeks to replace it with a 'religion of humanity'. Her novels are the profoundest examination of the nineteenth-century individual in relation to his or her environment and, in their consistent working out of her religious humanism in action, the greatest fictional embodiment of any philosophical position in the language.

George Eliot was the most intellectual of all English novelists, but there is nothing drily pedantic about her fiction, because of her large stylistic resources and her full command of the narrative, dramatic and descriptive techniques inherited from writers like Scott, Austen (whom she was strangely reluctant to appreciate), Charlotte Brontë and Trollope—all in their various ways deeply concerned with their characters' actions and responsibilities within their communities. George Eliot's greatness as a novelist-thinker lies in her skill in producing fiction as realistic and as readable as theirs, and yet at the same time dramatising one of the most interesting Victorian answers to the problems raised by scientific advances and religious doubt in an age of rapid social change.

She did not, however, become the intellectual historian of her age without displaying evidence of strenuous thinking, and certain readers then and since have complained that the imaginative element in her novels has sometimes foundered in the analysis— or, as it was put 100 years ago, the characters have been destroyed under dissection. She was deeply aware of how damaging it would be to neglect the realistic level of fiction for philosophical 'message', and in a letter to Frederic Harrison in 1866 she wrote of 'the severe effort of trying to make certain ideas thoroughly incarnate, as if they had revealed themselves to me first in the flesh and not in the spirit'. So her intention was to convey ideas, but must appear to be principally the presentation of a recognisable world. Properly managed—and she rejected blatant didacticism—a realistic work of literature was more revealing than any other about human existence, or more 'instructive', as the mid-Victorians would have said, since they always discussed their art in terms of moral teaching. George Eliot dignified the novel by raising it to the level of poetry, tragedy or philosophy in the minds of her contemporaries, through her high moral seriousness.

Having condemned overt didacticism in her letter to Harrison, she goes on to put what in mid-Victorian terms is the highest claim for realistic art:

> I think aesthetic teaching is the highest of all teaching because it deals with life in its highest complexity. But if it ceases to be purely aesthetic—if it lapses anywhere from the picture to the diagram—it becomes the most offensive of all teaching.

Although her fictional picture nowhere degenerates into diagram, her own criterion makes *Middlemarch* (1871–2) her greatest novel, for there her ideas are most perfectly clothed in realistic action, whereas an allegorical structure is easily diagnosed in *Adam Bede* (1859) or *Silas Marner* (1861), or even in *The Mill on the Floss* (1860).

Moral purity, 'truth-to-life' and 'elevation' were the qualities most prized by mid-Victorian critics of the novel, though no amount of the second would compensate for a want of the first, and many a writer's choice of subject was held to offend what Thackeray called 'my squeamish public', or, as Dickens's embodiment of bourgeois philistinism, Mr Podsnap, put it, 'to bring a blush to the cheek of the Young Person'. 'That such things are . . . [is] no sufficient reason for describing them in a novel', said a typical critic of the 1860s, echoing the phrasing and the opinion of Samuel Johnson a century before. By realistically treating the mid-century crisis of faith, George Eliot not only won a large and sympathetic following but managed to satisfy her serious critics' longing for 'truth' and 'elevation' as well as morality.

George Eliot—or more properly Marian Evans, since she adopted her pen-name only for her fiction—was deeply involved in developments which demolished one of the props of orthodox Christianity by denying the divine inspiration of the scriptures, reinterpreting them as historical documents and as ethical teaching instead of the word and law of God. In 1846 she published her translation of David Strauss's *Life of Jesus*, which put a mythical and historical human figure in place of a divinity. During the 1840s she had turned from the evangelism of her up-bringing to a kind of deism, and in the 1850s she moved farther when she came under the influence of thinkers like T. H. Huxley, G. H. Lewes and Herbert Spencer, who abandoned Christianity but were intent on constructing a humanistic simulacrum of Christian morality on agnostic, 'scientific' principles, renouncing a received religion they could no longer believe, yet not positively embracing atheism.

Alarmed at what might be the consequences for human life of adopting a view of a godless universe, various thinkers of the day tried to compensate for the loss of the supernatural by something akin to Feuerbach's 'religion of humanity', or Comte's institutionalised social religion on secular lines. George Eliot herself retained a strongly religious mind all her life, combining such modern scientific and philosophical doctrines as would support traditional morality and guarantee for the individual conscience and consciousness a key place in the scheme of things. Under such a system, moral imperatives like honesty and duty were supposedly derived from purely natural circumstances, and love and reverence likewise stemmed from and should be directed towards human individuals and institutions.

It is a version of this humanistic position that George Eliot presents in her first novel, *Adam Bede*, which demonstrates that the moral life is to be lived by avoiding one-sided human development, because it is not to be found either in worldliness or in over-spiritual religion, but only in a religious life that is engaged in the world. Egotism, which shows an arrested moral development, is the one unforgivable sin, since it precludes disinterested love of one's fellow men. Meanwhile the dominant animal-imagery constantly reminds us of man's animal nature, but also of his ability—indeed his duty—to transcend it. Admittedly the framework of ideas in the novel is highly schematic, yet, despite the very obvious signification of the characters and the action, the fiction is strong enough at the realistic level to carry the weight imposed on it.

In George Eliot's subsequent novels there is an increasing

awareness of the community, as she enlarges her cast and applies more complicated social and family pressures on her characters. In *The Mill on the Floss* Maggie Tulliver's development is brilliantly traced in terms of her sense of self as well as parental influences, family ideology, and the forces of a narrow provincial society, to make this a fine example of the Victorian concern with the psychology of the individual in relation to the environment. This two-fold attention to the inner and outer aspects of character led novelists as different as Gaskell, Trollope, George Eliot and Meredith to anticipate many of the findings of psychoanalysis, and to develop for their own use a range of techniques for rendering simultaneous thought and speech or thought and action, such as incorporating 'submerged speech' or 'submerged thought' in the stream of narrative, as Jane Austen had done before them.

The mid-Victorian ideal was to examine the personal and the social aspects of life in a setting of cosmic and religious speculation. Thus *Adam Bede* was highly acceptable, and so was *Silas Marner* later on, because it was based on a clear moral parable about achieving a balance between earthly and heavenly riches in human love. On the other hand, at least one critic revealed a worry lest the claustrophobic atmosphere of *The Mill on the Floss* represented a distraction of attention from transcendental considerations and a down-valuing of the individual's place in the universe. George Eliot was trying to work out the dialectic between the claims of the self and the 'other', towards a synthesis centring on the individual's responsibility for his or her own character and actions.

A primary impulse of nineteenth-century humanism was to maintain a high valuation of the individual vis-à-vis society and vis-à-vis the cosmos, at a time when scientific determinism threatened to show mankind as the victim of circumstances and devoid of free will or moral responsibility. Thackeray had displayed mankind as morally frail, scarcely responsible and more than a little ridiculous, while only late in his career did Dickens produce individual psychological studies sufficiently deep and extended to constitute investigations of personal responsibility, as he examined it, for example, in Pip in *Great Expectations* or Eugene Wrayburn in *Our Mutual Friend*. For his part, Trollope displayed the individual as 'invaded' by the world—as his contemporaries saw it—unable to preserve a central core of personality in the face of worldly pressures, and hence 'the creature of circumstances, led by temporary aims, rather than in that attitude of defying and controlling them, which constitutes the hero'. George Eliot's solution was to consider the individual to be caught in the 'web' of society, within a cosmos ruled by deterministic laws, but still to retain full responsibility for his actions and choices, which have 'an indestructible life both in and out of our consciousness' (*Romola*, chapter 16). Mankind is free because we are empowered to form our own moral nature by 'the re-iterated choice of good or evil that gradually determines character' (*Romola*, chapter 23). In her fiction, psychological motivation is part of causality, and if enough could be known about circumstances at any given moment—including the motives and character of each person involved—subsequent events would be seen to be determined, partly through each individual's exertion of will. But other people's motives cannot be identified and any full explanation is necessarily fictional, so that the novelist has an advantage over the philosopher in being allowed to analyse what the philosopher knows to be unknowable. This is what George Eliot meant in her letter to Frederic Harrison in saying that 'aesthetic teaching is the highest of all teaching because it deals with life in its highest complexity'. The omniscient author is playing God in her fictional world and offering to show the reader beneath the surface of an apparently 'true-to-life' society, the secrets of which must necessarily remain unknown in real life. (Readers exasperated by George Eliot's authorial manner may be reacting against even a temporary surrender of control to an Almighty.)

Fictional models of human conduct remain fresh in their complexity, even to those who do not share the modes of thought which underlie them and, although materialism is not an emotional threat today and Christians have re-formed themselves against the assault of science, George Eliot's fiction will continue to work suggestively to every age as a picture of human character and conduct, as well as a historical register of her period. Her fiction after all expresses the tragic sense of life lived in response to inner desires and aspirations, in a universe in which the operation of the laws of causality perpetually frustrates them. This feeling recurs in western culture and, in her particular case, is supported by the nineteenth-century positivistic vision of a universe governed by an inexorable scientific order, in which the individual retains the impulse to transcend his limitations and the freedom to attempt to do so. In the past, Christianity satisfied these human aspirations by turning worldly defeats into other-worldly triumphs, but the loss of faith to George Eliot meant 'to do *without opium* and live through all our pain with conscious, clear-eyed endurance'. She was left with only so much hope as she could find in humanity and 'a rooted conviction . . . that the immediate object and the proper sphere for all our highest emotions are our struggling fellow-men and this earthly existence'.

This did not mean abandoning Christianity as a proper concern in fiction, since to the positivist it was the product of the natural moral order of human life and the highest part of the historical, cultural tradition—hence its centrality in an agnostic's novels, and hence the clergymen and religious devotees in which they abound. George Eliot translated *The Essence of Christianity* by the German materialist, Ludwig Feuerbach, who maintained that religious conceptions of God were objectifications or externalisations of the highest aspects of human nature, so that studying religious life was a way of investigating the best in mankind. In *The Mill on the Floss* she posits that morality and religion are products of a correct understanding of the deterministic order of the world, and she shows Maggie prostrated by sorrow because she lacks 'that knowledge of the irreversible laws within and without her, which, governing the habits, becomes morality, and developing the feelings of submission and dependence, becomes religion' (IV.iii, Everyman, p269).

Moral law, as presented in *Romola* (1862–3), is the evolutionary product of human life, based on sentiments 'which the complicated play of human feelings had engendered in society' (chapter 11, Everyman, pp113–14). In the struggle for survival, thinkers like Spencer believed, those societies prospered best in which the individual members showed the largest amount of altruistic love for their fellows. In this way the evolution of civilisation from savagery, it was hoped, paralleled the evolution of man from animal, on the assumption that it was the power to love and cherish other members of the species that separated men from animals, and had given the species its evolutionary advantage in the struggle for life. Human nature—naturally evolved but invariable over any short historical span—is therefore the proper study of mankind and must be examined in terms of the stream of history. In the 'Proem' to *Romola*, George Eliot pictures the 'angel of dawn' flying over Europe in 1492, and compares what it sees with things in her own day:

> The great river courses which have shaped the lives of men have hardly changed; and those other streams, the life-currents that ebb and flow in human hearts, pulsate to the same great needs, the same great loves and terrors . . . [W]e are impressed with the broad sameness of the human heart, which never alters in the main headings of its history—hunger and labour, seed-time and harvest, love and death.
>
> (Everyman, p1)

What fascinated her in fifteenth-century Florence was 'its strange web of belief and unbelief' and of Christianity and classical learning, in the context of which she could trace the stages in Tito Malema's neglect of natural, filial duty, against 'Romola's self-repressing colourless young life, which had thrown all its passion into sympathy with aged sorrows, aged ambition, aged pride and indignation', and could set Romola's brother's religion, which 'places visions before natural duties' against

Savonarola's, 'whose preaching never insisted on gifts to the invisible powers, but only on help to visible need'. Finally Romola drifts over the sea in 'a new baptism', and tends a plague-stricken village in the likeness of a new Madonna, ending the novel in preaching stoicism and duty, and tending little children, who are in all ages symbolic of 'the eternal marriage between love and duty'.

George Eliot told her best contemporary critic, Richard Holt Hutton, that *Romola* was addressed to 'minds prepared not simply by instruction, but by that religious and moral sympathy with the historical life of man which is the larger half of culture'. This view of culture, which found its most famous expression in Matthew Arnold and is still heard from twentieth-century humanists today, seeks to justify George Eliot's type of fiction as one of the highest literary forms. It explains, too, the central role of what in a lesser writer might have been mere setting, background or costume for the characters—that is, the mass of historical and artistic material which she incorporates into her picture of Florentine life, and which has slowed down the novel so much for many readers that it must be judged a brilliant failure. Her English scenes were more familiar and easier to establish; they required less erudition and allowed more humour, but their function is the same—to show the individual immersed in the stream of history:

> It is the habit of my imagination to strive after as full a vision of the medium in which a character moves as of the character itself. The psychological causes which prompted me to give such details of Florentine life and history as I have given, are precisely the same as those which determined me in giving the details of English village life in 'Silas Marner,' or the "Dodson" life, out of which were developed the destinies of poor Tom and Maggie.

It is characteristic of the thought of that age of limited democracy and competitive capitalism to lay the fullest possible emphasis on the role of the individual in the social and historical process.

George Eliot did not entirely break with this general approach, and history as seen in *Romola* was the sum of innumerable people's individual deeds and desires, while her next novel, *Felix Holt the Radical* reaffirmed her belief in the individual, this time in the context of the modern class struggle. This novel demonstrates her political conservatism, which is the outcome of her systematic thought. This in itself, though it was advanced in the context of bourgeois ideology, can be seen as reactionary in the light of historical movement, because her wish to turn 'Class Interests into Class Functions or duties', ignores the realities of power. It also equates the aspirations of a whole class with competitive individualism, which she reacted against as a threat to tear apart 'the fine widespread network of society in which [the individual] is fast meshed'.

Felix Holt contained her largest social picture to date, from the very opening account of an imaginary coach-ride away from the agricultural south into the industrial Midlands, yet is more successful in treating the dilemmas of individual morality than large social movements. Her next novel is her greatest statement of the Victorian compromise between individual aspirations and social facts. Indeed *Middlemarch* is the most carefully worked out social model in English fiction, and is firmly rooted in the years which truly established the character of the Victorian age, just before the queen's accession. This was a time of religious controversy and German Higher Criticism, political agitation and reform, railway building, and rapid advances in the study of the physiological bases of life. All these George Eliot brings into complicated play in a novel which shows no sign of having been forced into shape merely to illustrate certain more-or-less positivist principles.

Her final novel shows less secure intellectual control, for she abandons the philosophical basis of *Middlemarch* and instead builds on Matthew Arnold's distinction between Hellenic and Hebraic strands in western culture. In a way which would have appalled her earlier positivist self, she allows characters to have intuitions as to their destinies, and act—with authorial approval—in response to the promptings of racial memory or transcendent influences of some sort. Yet *Daniel Deronda* (1876) contains very fine scenes analysing English landed society and, if it is a sort of failure, it is so only in relation to the immense success of *Middlemarch*.

CHAPTER 10

New Approaches
Meredith, Hardy and Butler

In the mid-century, the ideal vision of man was as the master of circumstances, not their victim, but struggling, with or without divine help, for control over his own destiny. Writers as different as Defoe and Sterne came under Victorian disapproval, the first for having undermined individual responsibility by his stress on external 'necessity' as a factor in human action, and the latter for illustrating the inadequacy of human understanding, and displaying man as the comic victim of elaborate concatenations of circumstances. Part of the resistance Thackeray's satire met sprang from revulsion at his vision of the world in which human beings were degraded to the status of puppets. George Eliot, on the other hand, made the most detailed and philosophical examination to be found in the literature, of personal responsibility in a complex world where human knowledge is necessarily limited. Yet, however interconnected people may be in her fictional societies, her central values are all individual, and all pertain to *personal* duty, responsibility, sense of self, and so on.

A recognition of gesture as communication led writers from Richardson to James to place great significance on small-scale action, and in Austen and Trollope there can be seen in addition an awareness of social behaviour and gesture as forming an expressive or communicative system, a 'language of manners' as one critic called it. To be exploited by the novelist, this 'language' must either be readily comprehensible to the reader—so that fictional characters and public ought ideally to belong to a fairly restricted segment of society—or it must be susceptible of rapid elucidation in which new light can wittily be thrown on motives and actions. In extreme cases, conventions can be seen not only to guide or restrict the individual character's deeds but to take control, so that, given a sufficiently unheroic set of dramatis personae, the social dance will carry them away through its established steps. Dickens burlesques this social process at the Podsnaps' dance in *Our Mutual Friend* when

> sixteen disciples of Podsnappery went through the figures of—1, Getting up at eight and shaving close at a quarter past—2, Breakfasting at nine—3, Going to the City at ten—4, Coming home at half-past five—5, Dining at seven, and the grand chain.
>
> (chapter 11, PEL, p184)

One of the most extraordinary visions of life as a game is found in Trollope's *The Way We Live Now* (1874–5), which concerns the operation of speculative capitalism in a world from which human values and emotions have been banished. People are turned to stone and reduced to a state of total alienation, which is the price Trollope shows the world paying for its worship of money—or rather, of credit, since no actual money ever changes hands, as bills have replaced cash in the City, while a drinking and gambling club, the Beargarden, which provides a moral parallel to the City in the novel, survives precariously on the exchange of worthless IOUs. This is Thackerayan satire applied to an up-to-date subject, but without Thackeray's sentimental indulgence, and with more of distaste than delight at human nature. It is possible to see Thackeray in terms of a continued contradiction between the humour of sympathy and the heart, and the intellectual enjoyment of incongruity which is called 'wit'. The author of *The Way We Live Now* has no sympathy with the objects of his attack, and his disgust at their vices finds no relief in laughter.

GEORGE MEREDITH

The Victorian writer in whom, more than anyone else, wit came to a new flowering was George Meredith. In one respect it is not a large step from the social games and strategies of Trollope's comedies, like *The Small House at Allington* or *The Eustace Diamonds*, to Meredith's vision of life as absurd play (though neither writer would have relished the association). Meredith transfers his attention from the individual to the system—the codes and conventions of behaviour—leaving the individual pretentiously to act out his part, watched by the 'imps' of comedy. From another point of view, the gap between most mid-Victorians and Meredith is huge and, as much as anything else, involves the admission of intellectual play into the novel. Certainly George Eliot was intellectual, but she was also both deeply serious and profound in her humour too, hence avoiding lapses in Victorian eyes, while Meredith not only enjoyed wit for its own sake, but used it to discredit great British institutions. Trollope's social comedy was largely descriptive and explanatory of the language of manners, and was therefore usually acceptable in his age. Meredith pushed the analysis farther to a fundamental critique of ruling-class values.

Recognition of Meredith was slow. For one thing he was too 'difficult' for many novel-readers, and as late as 1895—thirty-nine years after his first novel—an important but conservative critic complained of him in the *Edinburgh Review*: 'We have always maintained that the primary function of novel-writing is to entertain, and that no novelist has the right to demand such severe and sustained effort,' Two favourable comments by George Gissing in 1885 further elucidate the difficulties Meredith faced:

> It is amazing that such a man is so neglected. For the last thirty years he has been producing work unspeakably above the best of any living writer and yet no one reads him outside a small circle of highly cultured people. Perhaps that is better than being popular, a hateful word.

[*Diana of the Crossways*] is right glorious . . . but, mind you, to be read twice, if need be thrice. There is a preface, which is a plea for philosophic fiction . . . More 'brain stuff' in the book, than many I have read for long.

Meredith was one of the first British novelists for whom an absolute split appeared in the educated novel-reading public, between the high-brow literati and the rest. It must be acknowledged that hardly any of the novelists mentioned in this book were ever read by more than a small section of the population, and even Dickens's substantial sales figures were dwarfed by those of a truly popular writer like G. W. M. Reynolds. Meredith did not even attract the broad middle-class public of a Trollope or a George Eliot, for he tended to undermine standard Victorian orthodoxies by attacking accepted notions of religion, gentility, sexual morality, the status of women, national pride and, not least, the utility and high moral seriousness of art.

The Ordeal of Richard Feverel (1859) concerns Sir Ausin Feverel's misjudged and unsuccessful education of his son according to a document of his own, which he has entitled 'The Pilgrim's Scrip', and intends as the perfect system to produce purity in manhood. Exiled nature returns at the run, as Richard falls victim to a series of women, including 'Mrs Malediction', or Fate, and contracts an ultimately disastrous case of the 'Apple-Disease'. It is a highly selfconscious novel, while *The Egoist* (1879) goes even farther in deliberate 'artificiality', its fifty chapters' action being immersed in a discussion of the function of comedy as a stimulant to the mind and imagination, and a force for change. The authorial voice asserts that an attempt at 'copyism', or

conscientious transcription of all the visible, and a repetition of all the audible, is mainly accountable for our present branfulness, and that prolongation of the vasty and the noisy, out of which, as from an undrained fen, streams the malady of sameness, our modern malady.

(Prelude, PEL, p34)

On the other hand, comedy thrives on the remarkable, the eccentric and the self-deceived. Meredith's most famous novel takes the form of illustrated readings from 'a certain big book, the biggest book on earth . . . whose title is the Book of Egoism, and it is a book full of the world's wisdom' (Prelude, PEL, p33).

Comedy of a certain sort flourishes on the sex-war—as it did on the Restoration stage—for the 'love-season is the carnival of egoism' (chapter 11, PEL, p150) and, as it is male egoism Meredith finds expressed in the courtship dances of the human species, he reasonably adopts what for his age is a strikingly feminist position on women's rights to independence, property and meaningful social freedom. *Diana of the Crossways* (1885) is, one must agree with Gissing, one of his finest novels, and a very effective piece of feminist propaganda in comic guise. He is at his best when celebrating the 'newly enfranchised individuality' of his heroines, for he is not a reformer of institutions so much as an exposer of human impulses, actions and reactions that have been deformed in the mould of social convention, and he is the enemy of hypocritical intolerance, which, he optimistically says, 'holds the day, but not the morrow'.

Sir Willoughby Patterne, in the title role of *The Egoist*, is society's model of the ideal man, as he is described by society's representative:

> 'Rich, handsome, lordly, influential, brilliant health, fine estates,' Mrs Mountstuart enumerated . . . as there started across her mind some of Willoughby's attributes for the attraction of the soul of woman.
>
> (chapter 35, PEL, p428)

He aims at perfection in all things, like a would-be nineteenth-century Sir Charles Grandison, but in fact represents the insecurity at the heart of the ruling class, and is a ludicrous prisoner of the sex-conventions imposed by society.

This is disrespectful art, in which the description of 'the average Englishman' as 'excelling as a cavalier, a slayer, and an orderly subject', is not to be laughed at complacently, as at the equivalent *Punch* cartoon of the period, because elsewhere the author's voice takes on a more dangerous tone: 'English women and men feel toward the quick-witted of their species as to aliens, having the demerits of aliens—wordiness, vanity, obscurity, shallowness, and empty glitter, the sin of posturing' (*Diana*, chapters 6 and 11). Here is Meredith, the English-born Welshman, establishing a conspiracy of superiority with his enlightened readers over the English philistines who will not accept him.

A good example of Meredith's sympathetic exploitation of leading systems of thought occurs in *The Egoist*, when Clara Middleton has just looked down at Vernon Whitford (a thorough positivist, based in part on Leslie Stephen) who is dozing under a wild cherry tree:

> Looking upward, not quite awakened out of a transient doze, at a fair head circled in dazzling blossom, one may temporize awhile with common sense, and take it for a vision after the eyes have regained direction of the mind. Vernon did so until the plastic vision interwound with reality alarmingly . . . He jumped to his feet, rattled his throat, planted firmness on his brows and mouth, and attacked the dream-giving earth with tremendous long strides, that his blood might be lively at the throne of understanding.
>
> (chapter 12, PEL, p156)

Meredith's stories have indeed to be read 'with the head', but none the less he produced intensely emotional and dramatic scenes, such as chapter 26 of *Diana of the Crossways* which takes place while Emma's operation is happening off-stage. He developed further various ways of absorbing snatches of many different conversations into his narrative flow, and of rendering dialogue economically, with all its illogicalities and misunderstandings. He was reacting against the insipidity of 'drawing-room fiction', while pushing its methods further to new successes, and —just as Oscar Wilde did in the drama—was using established conventions to express his criticism of a society which, despite himself, as a man and a writer, he could not help enjoying.

THOMAS HARDY

By a quite insignificant irony of fate, it was Meredith who advised the young Thomas Hardy on how best to achieve success with the novel-reading public. His formula—uncongenial both to Hardy and himself—was tight plotting. Hardy could not, any more than Meredith himself, tie his creativity down to the tangling and untangling of a sensational plot, such as would arouse the instinct of the chase in the reader, for the pursuit of the resolution. Hardy's story-lines were significant in a quite different way, and in his greatest novels evoked expectations of fatality rather than exciting interest with 'mystery, enlargement, surprise, and moral obliquity'. Instead, events in his novels dramatise the place of mankind in the cosmic scheme of things—and Hardy's is a distinctively post-Darwinian universe.

Hardy could not accept a theologically minded modernist like Matthew Arnold, but absorbed instead the more advanced scientific thinkers, such as Herbert Spencer, and followed his own melancholy disposition into a pessimistic brand of determinism. Nearly all Victorian agnostics and atheists sought comfort for the loss of their deity: some, like George Eliot, adopting a compensatory 'religion of humanity' or, like Arnold, a belief in culture and tradition even more satisfactory to the reverential mind. Samuel Butler, among others, tried to flee from the apparent planlessness of Darwinism into a purposive evolutionism, but, rather than adopt this comfortable substitute for God's guiding hand, Hardy gradually turned for negative consolation to a kind of fatalism, which left the individual with pain, endurance and anger, but relieved him or her of the burdens of responsibility and freedom. An 'Immanent Will' is increasingly seen to guide events in his later novels, and his determinism—which, after all, does not posit a known end but only a chain of causality—is supplemented, as a literary device, with this fatalism of his, which suggests that somewhere there is a superior power that knows the future, like 'the President of the Immortals' who 'sports' with Tess. As regards the course of events, determinism and fatalism may come to the same thing, but as attitudes to life, they are very different, the former positing that all occurrences, including human actions, have their place in an unbroken chain of causes and effects, while the latter implies that our lot has been fixed beforehand by the resolution of some prescient power. By exploiting the literary possibilities of fatalism—and the omniscient narrator of a completed action in the past inevitably has quasi-divine knowledge of his story—Hardy rescues the individual from the status of simple victim, and endows him or her with all the dignity of the Greek tragic protagonist, face-to-face with the forces of the cosmos. In this way, Hardy's literary pessimism is its own comfort.

In an early poem, 'Hap', of 1866, he shows his desire for the kind of malignant but comforting fatality he embodies in his action of twenty-and-more years later:

> If but some vengeful god would call to me
> From up the sky, and laugh: 'Thou suffering thing,
> Know that thy sorrow is my ecstasy,
> That thy love's loss is my hate's profiting!'
>
> Then would I bear it, clench myself, and die,
> Steeled by the sense of ire unmerited;
> Half-eased in that a Powerfuller than I
> Had willed and meted me the tears I shed.

In *A Pair of Blue Eyes* (1873), a scientist, Knight, is clinging to a cliff and in his perilous, exposed position he begins to adopt the thinking of the 'musing weather-beaten West-country folk who pass the greater part of their days and nights out of doors', and who regard Nature

as a person with a curious temper; as one who does not scatter kindnesses and cruelties alternately, impartially, and in order, but

heartless severities or overwhelming generosities in lawless caprice.
(chapter 22, New Wessex Paperback Edition, p241)

Knight's previous rationalism cannot stand up to the extremity
he is now in and, because '[w]e colour according to our moods the
objects we survey', he as a character for the moment takes on the
Wessex belief in the malignancy of nature, which Hardy the
novelist exploits so thoroughly in his later novels:

> We are mostly accustomed to look upon all opposition which is
> not animate as that of the stolid, inexorable hand of indifference,
> which wears out the patience more than the strength. Here, at any
> rate, hostility did not assume that slow and sickening form. It was
> a cosmic agency, active, lashing, eager for conquest: determina-
> tion; not an insensate standing in the way.
>
> (chapter 22, New Wessex Paperback Edition, p242)

This is a case of fatalism psychologically colouring determinism
when Knight is at the limits of survival, until at last he cannot
help pondering, as though he were significant in the evolutionary
scheme, why *he* should be dying in this arbitrary fashion, and his
intelligence be lost to the world, when 'such an experiment in
killing might have been practised upon some less developed life'.

In *Jude the Obscure* (1896), Sue Bridehead has at one time believed in a mechanistic universe in which

> the First Cause worked automatically like a somnambulist, and
> not reflectively like a sage . . . But affliction makes opposing
> forces loom anthropomorphously; and those ideas were now
> exchanged for a sense of Jude and herself fleeing from a persecutor.
>
> (VI.iii, New Wessex Paperback Edition, p362)

In *Jude*, with its apt references to Job, and in most of the novels of
the 1880s and 1890s, this sense of divine persecution dominates
the development of the story, bringing Hardy close to the
Shakespearian

> As flies to wanton boys, are we to the gods;
> They kill us for their sport
>
> (*King Lear*, IV.i, 36)

which is surely in his mind when, in his 1895 preface to *The Return of the Native* (1878), he imagines King Lear's agony acted out on the Wessex heathland he has described.

Prehistory, history and landscape are powerful presences in human lives in most of his novels, and the Celts, the Romans and the Doomsday surveyors still walk Egdon heath in memory. These presences never fade, but in the last novels they are joined by a more insistent awareness of social change, and a closer social and psychological analysis of the characters.

Even in a novel like *Under the Greenwood Tree* (1872), which shows the least troubled world in all Hardy, he is examining rural change at a significant moment, when the village church musicians are finally replaced by an organ imported from outside. The world is constantly changing according to laws of social evolution, so that the narrator of *The Return of the Native* can explain Diggory Venn, the reddleman, as being

> one of a class rapidly becoming extinct in Wessex, filling at present in the rural world the place which, during the last century, the dodo occupied in the world of animals. He is a curious, interesting, and nearly perished link between obsolete forms of life and those which generally prevail.
>
> (chapter 2, New Wessex Paperback Edition, pp37–8)

By *Tess of the D'Urbervilles* (1891), change is more insistent. Hardy's Wessex was never a timeless, idyllic place, but the home of the Tolpuddle Martyrs, and all degrees of rural happiness and unhappiness, unfalsified by the pastoral tradition or the shocked and superficial philanthropy of the literary specialists in country misery. In *Tess*, old families have fallen and new families have taken their place and their names; the railway now carries milk up to London breakfast-tables, while traditional rhythms of work are suddenly destroyed by the steam-driven threshing-machine, 'the red tyrant . . . which, whilst it was going, kept up a despotic demand upon the endurance of [the women's] muscles and nerves' (chapter 4, New Wessex Paperback Edition, p372). Tess herself has an education and attitudes which separate her radically from her parents' generation, and she has a command of so-called 'standard' English in addition to her native dialect.

When it comes to *Jude the Obscure*, the two main characters are both analysed in even greater social and psychological depth, and both are socially highly problematical. Jude Fawley, the stone-mason, has obtained an education, but not, of course, through the approved, establishment channels, and expresses his bitter sense of exclusion from 'Christminster' (or Oxford), by chalking a quotation from the Book of Job on the walls of Biblioll College: 'I have understanding as well as you; I am not inferior to you: yea, who knoweth not such things as these?' (*Jude*, II.vi, New Wessex Paperback Edition, p138). His cousin, Sue Bridehead, is an advanced, emancipated girl of the time, who distrusts marriage as 'a trap' and views it with a pessimism learnt from the unhappy history of her and Jude's family:

Jude, do you think that when you *must* have me with you by law, we shall be so happy as we are now? The men and women of our family are very generous when everything depends upon their goodwill, but they always kick against compulsion. Don't you think it is destructive to a passion whose whole essence is its gratuitousness?

(V.iii, New Wessex Paperback Edition, pp290–1)

She feels an impulse towards sexual liberty, because love cannot always be given 'continuously to the chamber-officer appointed by the bishop's licence to receive it' (IV.i, p225). Out of line in her thinking with those around her, she faces sexual and social problems which at one point she tries to solve by bringing her body 'into complete subjection' (VI.viii, p408), with disastrous consequences.

Jude is Hardy's furthest development of social causality, and his subtlest account of the role of individual personality in the tragedy of life, since he began to work on this subject in *The Mayor of Casterbridge* (1886). Having abandoned standard Victorian individualism, he found a new way of examining the individual in relation to society, showing human life as hopeless, but finally rescuing man from insignificance by celebrating his struggle in art, and translating the unheroic victim of external forces into the hero of tragedy. Mid-Victorian critics waxed enthusiastic whenever a work of fiction approached the borders of tragedy, feeling that though this was acknowledged to be 'the age of the novel' the form had not yet been sufficiently dignified by its themes and subjects to reflect credit on the epoch. However, the tragedy they looked for, which should transform Mudie's library into the fifth-century Athenian theatre, was presumably expected to be altogether nobler than Hardy's, with bigger, weightier protagonists than his, and grander crimes and misfortunes than murders in lodging-houses, seductions, adder-bites, and a letter lost beneath a mat.

His considerable extension of fictional subject-matter ran counter to his contemporaries' yearnings for 'elevation' and 'idealisation', but was none the less part of that important Victorian tendency towards the serious treatment of 'humble' subjects to which Gaskell, Trollope and George Eliot contributed. In 1856 George Eliot had written, 'To make men moral, something more is requisite than to turn them out to grass'; it was Hardy who purged mindless pastoralism from English fiction, though a certain urban nostalgia—as in Gissing's *Demos* (1886) or *The Private Papers of Henry Ryecroft* (1903)—persisted for an imagined world of peace and innocence. One of Hardy's lighter novels, like *Under the Greenwood Tree*, might still be thought 'charming' and the near-caricatures that occur in his earlier fiction be taken for 'comic rustics', but in *Tess* the serious lyrical account of the happy life on Talbothays Farm, and the vivid picture of suffering and exploitation on the hard lands of Flintcomb Ash, raise not only the life of ordinary country people but the whole subject of daily work and manual labour into realistic fiction for more or less the first time, and connect the qualities of their existences firmly to economic factors like the type of land, the presence or absence of a landlord, and the system of employment.

To achieve this meant tackling once more the problem of dialect speech, to use it as a medium of serious communication and intelligent comedy, and not just the object of genteel mockery, and at the same time to make it comprehensible. In reply to a critic in 1878, Hardy said that he aimed to retain 'the idiom, compass, and characteristic expression' of the Dorsetshire dialect, without falling into the trap of spelling quaintly in order to represent regional pronunciation:

> In the printing of standard speech hardly any phonetic principle at all is observed; and if a writer attempts to exhibit on paper the precise accents of a rustic speaker he disturbs the proper balance of a true representation by unduly insisting upon the grotesque element; thus directing attention to a point of inferior interest, and diverting it from the speaker's meaning, which is by far the chief concern where the aim is to depict men and their natures rather than their dialect forms.

The story of the expansion of the social range of English fiction can be told in part in terms of a frequent and radical drive to 'depict men and their natures' outside the limits of the ruling class; examples may be cited in Defoe, Richardson, Scott, Dickens and Gaskell before Hardy; in Gissing and Moore, among his contemporaries, and Robert Tressell and D. H. Lawrence immediately after him. Hardy was left, however, with the problem of unintentionally distancing his characters socially because of a contrast between their modes of speech and the standard English of the authorial voice, so that the reader might come to believe that he or she was invited to share with this voice a 'superior' attitude to them. This was one of the considerations which led Lawrence to develop a new kind of narrative language in *The Rainbow*.

SAMUEL BUTLER

Some of Hardy's novels—especially *Tess* and *Jude*—offended contemporary moral opinion by their irreligion, as well as by the comparatively unveiled sexuality, which forced him to bowdlerise them for magazine serialisation. An even more shocking contemporary of his, who specialised in causing affronts by pointing to Victorian hypocrisy in questions of morals and religion, was Samuel Butler; like Hardy, he was closely interested in the latest developments in scientific thought, and his radical assault on Victorian ideologies even included an attack on some of the root assumptions of Darwinism. In one sense his approach paralleled Meredith's in that he moved away from a consideration of sets of morally responsible individuals and undertook instead an analysis of their modes of thought. He did not consider that the individual, however deeply probed, provided an adequate standard of reference for a critical examination of the world, and he laid stress less than most mid-Victorian thinkers on the resources of the single personality and more on the control exerted by genetic and environmental factors over human behaviour. The child, he thought, inherited character traits, abilities and experience from its biological forebears, and was powerfully formed or deformed by its upbringing as well. Since, in Butler's eyes, there was no suffering 'so awful as childhood in a happy united God-fearing family', his was clearly no timid gesture but a frontal attack on standard Victorian beliefs (*The Way of All Flesh*, PEL, p433).

His *Erewhon* (1872) is a brilliantly witty satire on nineteenth-century ideas, assumptions and institutions, and in particular on the optimistic myth of human and social progress. His great novel *The Way of All Flesh* is even more iconoclastic, but too full of individual attacks to be published until after his death, in 1903. It became a major text in the early-twentieth-century reaction against Victorianism, one of the most influential analyses of a repressive religious upbringing, and an important challenge to the authority of the paterfamilias and his heavenly paradigm. After many years and many mishaps, the protagonist finally emancipates himself from his background, and learns to see what shams are concealed by conventional religion, education, marriage and the family. Butler, whose life almost exactly coincided with Queen Victoria's reign, was one of the writers who radically undermined the security of commonplace Victorian views of the world.

CHAPTER 11

Late-Victorian Choices
James, Wilde, Gissing and Moore

The heterodoxies of Meredith, Hardy and Butler were distinctly British in inspiration and to a large extent developments of lines of thought which were present, though submerged, in the mid-Victorian period. It had been a period of monstrous middle-class self-confidence, and the novel, as the literary form which that class most exclusively possessed, had shared for a while in this comfortable self-complacency. A George Eliot was obviously a world away from the hateful philistines, yet at bottom she, too, subscribed to the same moral and individualistic premises as they did. The weakening of the hold of mid-Victorian moralism left novelists without a secure base from which to work, for the standard narrative, with its insistent moral commentary, so suitable for examining the great Victorian subjects of duty and responsibility, no longer satisfied fashionable ideas on art. It was necessary to appeal to the example of a literature which had an enviable history of revolt against moralistic and utilitarian standards in art, and had long perfected its techniques for shocking the bourgeoisie.

The French literary standards which made such an impact in Britain in the 1880s and 1890s came as an amalgam of ideas from very different schools of thought. Following in the footsteps of the painters whom Whistler had been sending over to Paris for a couple of decades, literary men fell suddenly in love with a semi-imaginary *vie de bohème* and gulped down without chronological discrimination fifty whole years of French protest against bourgeois philistinism, dating from Théophile Gautier's 1834 manifesto of 'art for art's sake' in the preface to his *Mademoiselle de Maupin* and continuing right up to the very latest naturalistic novel by Émile Zola. Thackeray had enjoyed Parisian life and society, but not with the great aesthetic excitement experienced by the characters of Henry James or recorded by George Moore in his autobiographical pieces and his first novel, *A Modern Lover* (1883). Paris had for some time been the scene of English dissipation for those who could afford to see whether indeed things sexual were ordered better in France than under the watchful eye of Mrs Grundy.

Matthew Arnold had taught that France had the culture while Britain had the morals, and in *Literature and Dogma* (1873) he had rhetorically asked '. . . which is the more vital concern for a man: conduct, or arts and antiquities?' (p235). The correct reply, of course, was 'conduct', but many artists and writers of the end of the century set about re-answering the question. Even Henry James made morality a matter of quasi-aesthetic sensitivity rather than obedience to natural or divine law, while in reaction to Victorian repressiveness certain other writers, like Wilde, deliberately traded in paradoxes and totally reversed Arnold's original answer.

The poet Arthur Symons, one of the central figures in creating the myth of the decadent '90s, explained the polar extremes in critical attitudes at the time, when he wrote, in the preface to the second edition of his *Silhouettes* in 1896, of two conflicting standpoints from which a work of art could be judged: 'the standpoint from which its art is measured entirely by its morality, and the standpoint from which its morality is measured entirely by its art'. To take a representative from the old-fashioned camp, George Eliot's most sympathetic critic, R. H. Hutton of the *Spectator*, survived into the 1890s, still wanting literature to show 'the indissoluble relation in which earthly life must for ever stand to both

Heaven and Hell', and championing the minor talent of William Watson as a 'healthy' poetic influence in an age of crumbling moral standards, but living to be reviled by Saintsbury for his mid-Victorian way of 'telling you what you *ought to* read, you know'. At the other extreme was Oscar Wilde, with his infamous aphorism from the preface to *The Picture of Dorian Gray* (1891): 'There is no such thing as a moral book or an immoral book. Books are well written, or badly written. That is all.'

Different figures of the late-nineteenth century adopted every conceivable position between these extremes of moral judgement and art for art's sake, but one thing all the modern writers had in common, whatever their moral attitudes, was the demand that they be allowed freedom to choose their own subject matter without social censorship. Yeats put the case in his *Autobiographies*:

> Science, through much ridicule and some persecution has won the right to explore whatever passes before its corporeal eye, and merely because it passes . . . Literature now demands the same right of exploration of all that passes before the mind's eye, and merely because it passes.

On the one hand, this demand refers to one of the most fashionable subjects of the last three decades of the century—the subconscious mind—and implies exposing the whole complex of sexual impulses which earlier generations had repressed as 'morbid' or unclean. On the other, this style of argument assumes a quasi-scientific notion of the role of literature (in an age when science was thought by both its friends and its enemies to proceed systematically, without 'inspiration'), as researching both mental life and certain social subjects which art had usually ignored. The idea of the writer as a scientific researcher is fallacious on many counts, of course, not least in ignoring that it is the artist himself who has invented the material which he then claims 'objectively' to investigate; but the emotive appeal of scientific 'disinterestedness' was thrilling to iconoclastic young writers, more than one of whom must have felt George Moore's enthusiasm on reading Zola's manifestoes of naturalism:

> The idea of a new art based upon science, in opposition to the art of the old world that was based on imagination, an art that should explain all things and embrace modern life in its entirety, in its endless ramifications, be, as it were, a new creed in a new civilisation, filled me with wonder, and I stood dumb before the vastness of the conception, and the towering height of the ambition.

This grand ambition was fed by news from the continent of exciting new happenings in the arts—in most branches of literature and the visual arts in France, in drama and the novel in Scandinavia, and in music-drama in Germany. Meanwhile the last decades of the century saw the start of the modern transformation in European man's sense of himself and his society, as psychoanalysis and sociology increasingly explored those inner and outer 'unknown regions' which artists too were claiming as their rightful territory.

Whatever the direction of any given writer's reaction against the standards of Victorianism, he is likely to agree with Lord Henry Wotton in Wilde's *Picture of Dorian Gray* that

> there is no literary public in England for anything except newspapers, primers, and encyclopaedias. Of all people in the world the English have the least sense of the beauty of literature.
>
> (PEL, p51)

And whatever social pose he may adopt, be it the aristocratic dandy, the *déclassé* artist, or the honorary member of the proletariat, it will be in disgust at the middle classes who 'are not modern'. Some writers try, like Hardy, to extend their art without extravagantly shocking middle-class sensibilities; for others, the happiest thing in the world to contemplate is *le bourgeois épaté*, like 'the tweeded tourist' in Beardsley's poem 'The Three Musicians' (1896), who at the sight of sexual dalliance,

> Red as his guide-book grows, moves on, and offers up
>   a prayer for France.

The most shock-inducing of all utterances in the period issued from the central group of contributors to *The Yellow Book* (1894–7), whose decadence involved reversing the accepted romantic and Victorian relation between artifice and nature, preferring the former as the product of the highest civilisation, which the latter at best could only be made to emulate, so that the artificial was regarded as more natural than the natural. George Moore, for example, wrote (in French, incidentally) that in his *Confessions of a Young Man* (1886) he had painted the cheeks of his subject, 'so that they might assume an exact resemblance to life'. All art was superior to nature in beauty, as all beauty was above utility.

The calculated offence to accepted standards, which masqueraded as a withdrawal from social and political questions, stood in a direct line of descent from Théophile Gautier and his associates, whose promotion of art as an end in itself had in fact been a direct political reaction against the bourgeois victory in the revolution of 1830. During most of the century, bourgeois art had triumphed in Britain, and when alternative forms eventually asserted themselves it was as a similar minority move to fight bourgeois ideology on a new terrain. Gautier's preface to *Mademoiselle de Maupin* retained its sting and application over the years in the assault on middle-class positions:

> There is nothing really beautiful except what cannot be used for anything; everything which is useful is ugly; because it is the expression of some need; and the needs of man are ignoble and disgusting, like his poor and infirm nature.—The most useful place in a house is the latrines.

The new British version of *l'art pour l'art* is Gautier and his followers imported into what Wilde called 'the native land of the hypocrite'.

Wilde's own *Picture of Dorian Gray* was a strange but brilliantly epigrammatic account of a life given over entirely to the pursuit of sensation under the 'poisonous' influence of Huysmans's

À rebours (1884), which was a sacred text in the religion of artificiality and 'unnatural' pleasure. Drugs, preternatural happenings, aesthetic affectations, and *instantanés* of slum and dockland scenes, all vividly presented with total disregard for orthodox moral sensibilities, make this one of the brightest spots in late-century fiction, but despite its attractiveness, the decadent myth must not be allowed to outshine other, more lasting developments in literature.

Foreign influences were felt, or examples invoked, in two broad areas: that of devotion to the art of fiction in terms of style, chronology, point of view and design, and in this the masters were Balzac, Flaubert and Turgenev; and that of the extension of permissible social and moral subject-matter, for which Flaubert, Maupassant and Zola were most cited, and for which there was a certain awareness of modern Scandinavian novelists like Strindberg and J. P. Jacobsen. (There have always been two Flauberts, as far as his followers have been concerned: the Flaubert of stylistic exactitude, searching for *le mot juste*, and the Flaubert who was prosecuted for the alleged indecency of *Madame Bovary* in 1857, and is thus regarded as lying behind the moral freedoms of naturalism.)

HENRY JAMES

The most important technician was Henry James, whose presence as an American in the British literary world was a sign that the novel was now becoming international. In fact, James's cultural origins made him readier consistently to adopt the tenets of the more aesthetically demanding French theoreticians, since, as he recognised, the New World was in a strategic position to select without inhibition from the older European cultures: '[W]e can now deal freely with forms of civilization not our own, can pick and choose and assimilate and in short (aesthetically) claim our property wherever we find it.'

Finding English novelists comparatively reticent about their craft, and seeing that the art of fiction was, as he put it, *discutable* in France, James not unnaturally attributed his abiding concern with technical matters to his apprenticeship with French masters. Many of the lessons he learnt under them were available from British writers too, less systematically, indeed, and hidden amongst grossly philistine utterances, but none the less there; so that in effect he shaped himself under the influence of Balzac and Flaubert rather than trusting to the haphazard examples of his no less important English forebears. Early in his career he 'nestled, technically . . . and with yearning, in the great shadow of Balzac', where he studied the use of significant description (very different from 'copy-ism') in the rendering of a world, how to cope with the 'eternal time-question' by summary and foreshortening for clarity or richness, and how to play 'the constructional game' by centring his interest largely on one character, whose consciousness—and he went far beyond Balzac in this—should in effect be the dramatic set for the principal action. These things can be seen in the insistence with which *The Portrait of a Lady* (1880–1) is structured to profit most from the mental action of the receptive, intelligent but sometimes misguided mind of Isabel Archer herself, with places and other characters developed in their importance for her, with something implied in addition by the authorial tone of voice and the imagery to allow the reader to see just that much farther than Isabel so as to understand the great irony of her mistaken choice. The reader can grasp—for example, from Osmond's preoccupation with art-objects—something of his moral nature that is hidden from Isabel until her long meditation over a dying fire (in chapter 42) which, rather than any physical happening, is the central action of the book.

For such purposes James needed to go beyond the techniques which Austen and various Victorians had developed for simultaneously presenting speech, thought and perceptions, with authorial commentary, and he followed Flaubert's exploitation of *le style indirect libre*, by creating a highly flexible style able to communicate a character's state of consciousness, as well as speech and significant perceptions, in one continuous flow, without disturbing the harmony of the prose. In this way he aimed to free the novel from what he saw as the burden of an acknowledged author giving an omniscient commentary, and to concentrate the reader's attention into the 'felt life' of the subject, while avoiding awkward jars between different narrative and dramatic modes. Of course, there could be no direct authorial moral judgement, and old-fashioned critics, like Hutton, felt that 'proportion' had been lost in this 'agnostic' art, in which 'Mr Henry James long ago rejected the idea that real life is intelligible and significant' —that is, definable and assessable against the standards of nineteenth-century humanism.

In a novel such as *The Ambassadors* (1903) we find passages like the following in James's fully developed late style, in which quick time-shifts economise on the description of sustained mental states, and a character is seen examining his own reactions and the significance of what he sees, when he is, in a way symbolic of the normal condition of the Jamesian individual, cut off from direct communication with the person he wishes to understand. In a box in a Paris theatre, Strether, who has been made aware that the whole cause of his journey from the United States, Chad Newsome, has just entered and sat beside him, is trying to accommodate himself to the completely changed, Europeanised younger man:

Our friend was to go over it afterwards again and again—he was going over it much of the time that they were together, and they were together constantly for three or four days . . . The fact was that his perception of the young man's identity—so absolutely checked for a minute—had been quite one of the sensations that count in life; he certainly had never known one that had acted, as he might have said, with more of a crowded rush. And the rush, though both vague and multitudinous, had lasted a long time, protected, as it were, yet at the same time aggravated, by the circumstance of its coinciding with a stretch of decorous silence. They couldn't talk without disturbing the spectators in the part of the balcony just below them; and it, for that matter, came to Strether—being a thing of the sort that did come to him—that these were the accidents of a high civilization; the imposed tribute to propriety, the frequent exposure to conditions, usually brilliant, in which relief has to await its time.

(I.ii, PEL, pp88–9)

It must be admitted that at his most complex, James can be irritating to read in his last novels and the characters can seem as though they are unable to act, simply because they are buried up to the armpits in the author's late style. In his terms this is not a valid objection, since he was seeking to abolish the Victorian distinction between action and character by equating the presentation of the one with the analysis of the other. Nevertheless his concentration in the individual mind because it is the only knowable thing marks him out from most earlier British fiction, which usually set itself to build up, however 'subjectively' and however the picture might be coloured by the perceiving eye, a solid fictional world. In this sense James serves as an introduction to certain important twentieth-century developments, but is also somewhat alien to the British tradition, having different kinds of links with American literature, in the context of which his concern with New World innocence in curious interaction with cultured European corruption has a wider set of significances. His mode of fiction is attuned to the aesthetic appreciation of the values of individual moral behaviour and finds the sensitive response to a felt need for altruism or self-sacrifice a beautiful event, while the greatest sense of evil surrounds deeds which violate the wholeness of other people, or threaten the cultural and artistic heritage. Though he produces a scintillating novel from the complicated interplay of all these factors in his most highly developed social comedy—*The Spoils of Poynton* (1897), for example—he is most at home examining, under exceptional conditions, the psychology of late-nineteenth-century American individualism.

At the same time it is not surprising to find that his methods are not adaptable to certain other ends and that, although he argued repeatedly for the artist's right to choose his own subject where he would, for all practical purposes his technique itself imposed severe bounds on his freedom. It was, for example, hard for him to deal with a character whose consciousness was not a fine instrument for registering nuances of experience, and articulating them to himself or herself in intelligent, educated terms, which would locate them within an aesthetic framework of western culture. It could not be enough for him that an author should be, like Fielding, 'handsomely possessed of a mind', if his central personage were not. Although *The Princess Casamassima* (1886) displays James's customarily intensive examination of psychological states, because of his fictional procedures it tells us rather less about one matter in which it claims to take an interest —working-class life in London—and hardly anything about another—revolutionary politics; both of these would have been a central concern for a mid-Victorian novelist. Henry James's gains involved some losses, too.

GEORGE GISSING

In the same year, 1886, George Gissing's *Demos, a Story of English Socialism* appeared, representing the diametric opposite from James in the fiction of the day. Although not Gissing's best, it is as carefully researched as all his novels, since he relied on just that ' "authentic" information' of which James tells us he felt no need in *Princess Casamassima. Demos* provides fascinating descriptions of changing rural and industrial landscapes, and of indoor and outdoor political meetings, and it presents sets of social attitudes through characters who are as much socially as psychologically defined. But it is structured around a plot in which love and inheritance play their old-fashioned parts, and it fails through serious inconsistencies in Gissing's attitudes, in as much as he seems to feel that he has successfully discredited socialism by showing his protagonist taking a socialist stance merely in order to further his own career. Often Gissing's mingled love and fear of change produce more fruitful tensions.

He was not, like James, one of the striking technical innovators of the age, but in terms of 'low' or 'daring' subject-matter he was among those whose aim, a disgusted Tennyson assumed, was to

> Paint the mortal shame of nature with the living hues of Art

and

> Set the maiden fancies wallowing in the troughs of Zolaism
> ('Locksley Hall Sixty Years After', 1886, ll. 140 and 145)

For the younger Gissing there was no future in withdrawing into aestheticism or into the highly individualistic art of Henry James, because he saw

> the necessary union between beauty in life and social reform. Ruskin despairs of the latter, and so can only look on by-gone times. Younger men (like W. Morris) are turning from artistic work to social agitation just because they fear that Art will be crushed out of the world as things are.

Gissing himself largely abandoned his early Radical reformism in a temporary escape into aestheticism, which ended in his adopting a stance of artistic 'integrity', or refusal to compromise on questions of decency or popularity. One of his finest novels, *New Grub Street* (1891), deals with the problem of the artist in bourgeois society. Reardon, who is an honest, talented writer, falls into poverty along with his family, because he is unacceptable to the business-minded literary world and—like Meredith—refuses to write down to the popular taste of the philistines.

By this time Gissing had become even more strongly antidemocratic than he was in *Demos*, and was seeking relief in artistic élitism for his sense of social alienation as a writer, in the same way as he periodically tried to find an anti-bourgeois social identity by involving himself in the working class. His attitude to the working class was a shifting complex of pity, contempt and sympathetic understanding. He was working in a period when writers were increasingly exploring the East End of London and revealing urban material which lay close at hand geographically, but which the changing configuration of the capital had hidden from West End and suburban eyes. At his best Gissing operated against social ignorance, but ended his career as an unattractively snobbish Tory, in the phase he described in *The Private Papers of Henry Ryecroft* (1903).

His best novel of working-class life, *The Nether World* (1889), is the first English fiction to draw a horizontal cut through society, rather than the more usual nineteenth-century vertical section which displays interconnexions between different social strata. In this, and in his careful avoidance of Victorian moral comment, he followed Zola, whose dispassionate, 'scientific' attitude he tried to emulate, but surrendered occasionally to his inherited English impulse to pass instructive comments on his fiction during the narrative. His presentation of a separate working-class community is distinctly modern and marks the demise in English literature of the nineteenth-century myth of the organic society.

GEORGE MOORE

George Moore made much more ado than Gissing about the French influences which led *him* to flout British moral conventions in his first novel, *A Modern Lover* (1883), and as a result he was credited with a very large role in the introduction of French methods into English fiction. Indeed, *A Modern Lover* appears greater from a historical than a critical point of view. As the story of a sexually charming but mediocre painter, it quite effortlessly introduces 'dangerous' subjects which hitherto had only been dealt with in an obviously 'sensational' fashion that was in a way less offensive than a blasé moral indifference. The painter of the period is a key moral and aesthetic figure, usually gallicised and bohemian, and in the forefront of artistic developments. George Moore skilfully presents the corrupting effect of social ambition on *his* artist, Louis Seymour, by making him a weak-minded, easy-going character, whose real sin is not just sexual dalliance and adultery, but his failure to take the sacred calling of art seriously enough, and his capitulation to the conservative standards of Academicism.

Esther Waters (1894) is Moore's masterpiece; in it he accomplishes the Zolaesque task of using an illiterate servant-girl as the heroine of a realistic work which recounts what he calls—in an old-fashioned aside he cannot resist—'an heroic adventure if one considers it: a mother's fight for the life of her child against all the forces that civilisation arrays against the lowly and the illegitimate'. The novel contains a well-written scene of childbirth, and, for the period, very explicit, almost Laurentian accounts of a man's sexual mastery over the heroine. She shares with many characters in Hardy and Gissing a feeling that 'we don't choose our lives, we just makes the best of them'—an attitude which necessarily banishes such figures from the Jamesian universe, but which the approach of these other novelists raises to a new dignity of stoical endurance and utterance.

Moore was characteristic of the late nineteenth century in indiscriminately absorbing French theories as different as naturalism and aestheticism, which were originally the slogans of opposed factions but were joined together in Britain in the fight against Victorian moralism. (As a result, terms like 'realism' and 'naturalism' lose much of their French application in English.) The modernist battle was largely fought on the moral front, owing to the overriding tendency of Victorian thought to reduce all questions to morality, so that Henry James's extensive writings about prose fiction were completely fresh in English, and it is not surprising that at one time he was held to have 'invented' criticism of the form, although it is also unfortunate that the particular utterances which were so serviceable at that moment should have been interpreted as the master's sanction to ignore the historical and ideological roots of the novel. Certainly too much attention to his strictures on his predecessors' narrative methods for some while distorted twentieth-century readings of the Victorian novel, and of self-conscious eighteenth-century fiction too. We can now, however, see that James was just one part of a complex nineteenth-century legacy to the twentieth, which was left with sets of choices to be made and positions to be negotiated between purely aesthetic concerns and documentary or polemical fiction; between seemingly 'innocent' forms and self-confessed literary contrivance; between regional fiction and a national fiction, and between both of these and an international traffic in the novel that would recognise no linguistic barriers.

Select Bibliography

Dyson, A. E. (ed). *The English Novel: Select Bibliographical Guides.* Oxford University Press, 1974

Allen, Walter E. *The English Novel: a Short Critical History.* Phoenix House, 1954; Penguin, 1970

Allott, Miriam. *Novelists on the Novel.* Routledge, 1959

Altick, Richard D. *The English Common Reader: a Social History of the Mass Reading Public.* University of Chicago Press, 1957

Booth, Wayne C. *The Rhetoric of Fiction.* University of Chicago Press, 1961

Campos, Christophe. *The View of France: from Arnold to Bloomsbury.* Oxford University Press, 1965

Cazamian, Louis. *The Social Novel in England, 1830–1850: Dickens, Disraeli, Mrs Gaskell, Kingsley.* 1903; translated from French by M. Fido, Routledge, 1973

Grover, Philip. *Henry James and the French Novel: a Study in Inspiration.* Elek, 1973

Harvey, W. J. *Character and the Novel.* Chatto, 1965

Hewitt, Douglas. *The Approach to Fiction: Good and Bad Readings of Novels.* Longman, 1972

Hough, Graham. *Image and Experience: Studies in a Literary Revolution.* Duckworth, 1960

Keating, Peter J. *The Working Classes in Victorian Fiction.* Routledge, 1971

Kettle, Arnold C. *An Introduction to the English Novel.* 2 vols, Hutchinson, 1951 and 1953

Kiely, Robert. *The Romantic Novel in England.* Harvard University Press, 1972

Knoepflmacher, U. C. *Religious Humanism and the Novel: George Eliot, Walter Pater, and Samuel Butler.* Princeton University Press, 1965

Kovačevći, Ivanka. *Fact into Fiction: English Literature and the Industrial Scene 1750–1850.* Leicester University Press, 1975

Leavis, F. R. *The Great Tradition: George Eliot, Henry James, Joseph Conrad.* Chatto, 1948; Penguin, 1972

Lodge, David. *The Language of Fiction: Essays in Criticism and Verbal Analysis of the English Novel.* Routledge, 1966

McKillop, Alan D. *The Early Masters of English Fiction.* University of Kansas Press, 1956; Constable, 1962

Miller, J. Hillis. *The Forms of Victorian Fiction: Thackeray, Dickens, Trollope, George Eliot, Meredith and Hardy.* University of Notre Dame Press, 1968

Page, Norman. *Speech in the English Novel.* Longman, 1973

Parker, A. A. *Literature and the Delinquent: the Picaresque Novel in Spain and Europe 1599–1753.* Edinburgh University Press, 1967

Paulson, Ronald. *Satire and the Novel in Eighteenth-Century England.* Yale University Press, 1967

Stang, Richard. *The Theory of the Novel in England 1850–1870.* Routledge, 1959

Tave, Stuart M. *The Amiable Humorist: a Study in the Comic Theory and Criticism of the Eighteenth and Early Nineteenth Centuries.* University of Chicago Press, 1960

Tillotson, Kathleen M. *Novels of the Eighteen-forties.* Oxford University Press, 1954

Tompkins, Joyce M. S. *The Popular Novel in England, 1700–1800.* Constable, 1932; Methuen, 1962

Van Ghent, Dorothy. *The English Novel: Form and Function.* Reinhart, 1956; Harper Torchbooks, 1961

Watt, Ian. *The Rise of the Novel: Studies in Defoe, Richardson and Fielding.* Chatto, 1957; Penguin, 1972

Williams, Raymond. *Culture and Society 1780–1950.* Chatto, 1958; Penguin, 1971

Williams, Raymond. *The English Novel from Dickens to Lawrence.* Chatto, 1970; Paladin, 1974

Index

THE RISE OF THE NOVEL
Ian Watt

In these studies of Defoe, Richardson, and Fielding, Ian Watt investigates the reasons why the three main early eighteenth-century novelists wrote in the way they did – a way resulting ultimately in the modern novel of the present day. The rise of the middle class and of economic individualism, the philosophical innovations of the seventeenth century, complex changes in the social position of women: these are some of the factors he finds underlying an age which produced the authors of *Robinson Crusoe*, *Pamela*, and *Tom Jones*.

'An important, compendious work of inquiring scholarship ... alive with ideas ... an academic critic who in lively and suggestive detail is able to assemble round his novelists the ideas and facts among which they worked' – V. S. Pritchett in the *New Statesman*

THE HISTORICAL NOVEL
Georg Lukács

In this study an eminent Hungarian critic brilliantly maintains that the classical form of the historical novel was forged by Sir Walter Scott in a direct continuation of the great realistic social novels of the eighteenth century. He follows his inquiry down to the works of such modern writers as Romain Rolland, Feuchtwanger, and Heinrich Mann.

'It is an inquiry into the nature of the historical novel rather than a history of the *genre*; and although, or because, it strictly adheres to Marxist doctrine and method, the book abounds in brilliant insights' – Martin Esslin in the *Spectator*

'The analysis of Scott may be, to readers in this country, the most valuable thing in the book, but there is much else besides. No one interested in the imaginative approach to history should miss this absorbing study, which will lead him to fresh consideration of such giants as Goethe, Flaubert, Balzac, Tolstoy and even Shakespeare' – C. V. Wedgwood in the *Daily Telegraph*

Literary Criticism in Penguins

THE USES OF LITERACY
Richard Hoggart

Mass literacy has opened new worlds to new readers. How far has it also been exploited to debase standards and behaviour? Have the magazines, books, and films 'for the million' proved on balance a social benefit or a social danger?

When he began his researches into what the 'masses' read about (and sing about) in these times, Richard Hoggart found that popular literature must be related to the life and values of the people for whom it is produced. Drawing partly from his own boyhood experience, he portrays in fascinating detail the working class of Northern England, and their assumptions, attitudes, and morals.

'Packed with vivid detail and written with deep feeling ... absorbing and important' – Raymond Mortimer

'Required reading for anyone concerned with the modern cultural climate' – *The Times Literary Supplement*

POPULAR LITERATURE
Victor E. Neuburg

The Gipsey Girl; or, the Heir of Hazell Dell and *Varney the Vampire; or, The Feast of Blood* were best-selling nineteenth-century tales that drew comments such as 'the vilest trash imaginable' from some sober contemporaries. Yet these novels, and their many precursors in the form of pamphlets, leaflets and illustrated broadsheets, had the significant effect of transforming a whole oral tradition into a written culture. Not until recently, however, has popular literature – both for its content and for the light it throws on its readers – been recognized and studied as a distinct social force.

In this book Victor E. Neuburg traces the development of that rich and fascinating literature and the impact upon it of social change, from the beginning of printing to the end of the nineteenth century.

The text is illustrated with woodcuts and engravings, and includes an extensive critical bibliography.

Raymond Williams

CULTURE AND SOCIETY

In *Culture and Society* Raymond Williams has traced the idea of culture as it has developed in Britain from 1780 to 1950, 'culture' being defined as 'right knowing and right doing' and considered throughout in its relation to society rather than in its purely artistic sense.

'Brave, intelligent, and disciplined . . . a most impressive work' – C. P. Snow

'Penetrating, lucid, objective, and also honestly engaged . . . the best reasoned plea that I have read for a common culture' – Angus Wilson

THE LONG REVOLUTION

In *The Long Revolution* Raymond Williams continues the inquiry he began so successfully in *Culture and Society*. Examining the gradual change which is coming over our political, economic, and cultural life, he lays special emphasis on the 'creative mind' in relation to our social and cultural thinking. After discussing the theory of culture he turns to a fascinating historical study of such institutions as education and the press, traces the development of a common language, and reveals the links between ideas, literary forms, and social history.

'Clear . . . positive . . . analytic, very intelligent' – Richard Hoggart

'The book I have been waiting for since 1945' – Richard Crossman

ENGLISH AND AMERICAN
LITERATURE IN PENGUINS

☐ *Emma* **Jane Austen**   £1.10

'I am going to take a heroine whom no one but myself will much like,' declared Jane Austen of Emma, her most spirited and controversial heroine in a comedy of self-deceit and self-discovery.

☐ *Tender is the Night* **F. Scott Fitzgerald**   £2.95

Fitzgerald worked on seventeen different versions of this novel, and its obsessions – idealism, beauty, dissipation, alcohol and insanity – were those that consumed his own marriage and his life.

☐ *The Life of Johnson* **James Boswell**   £2.25

Full of gusto, imagination, conversation and wit, Boswell's immortal portrait of Johnson is as near a novel as a true biography can be, and still regarded by many as the finest 'life' ever written. This shortened version is based on the 1799 edition.

☐ *A House and its Head* **Ivy Compton-Burnett**   £3.95

In a novel 'as trim and tidy as a hand-grenade' (as Pamela Hansford Johnson put it), Ivy Compton-Burnett penetrates the facade of a conventional, upper-class Victorian family to uncover a chasm of violent emotions – jealousy, pain, frustration and sexual passion.

☐ *The Trumpet Major* **Thomas Hardy**   £1.25

Although a vein of unhappy unrequited love runs through this novel, Hardy also draws on his warmest sense of humour to portray Wessex village life at the time of the Napoleonic wars.

☐ *The Complete Poems of Hugh MacDiarmid*

☐ Volume One   £8.95
☐ Volume Two   £8.95

The definitive edition of work by the greatest Scottish poet since Robert Burns, edited by his son Michael Grieve, and W. R. Aitken.

ENGLISH AND AMERICAN LITERATURE IN PENGUINS

☐ *Main Street* **Sinclair Lewis** £3.95

The novel that added an immortal chapter to the literature of America's Mid-West, *Main Street* contains the comic essence of Main Streets everywhere.

☐ *The Compleat Angler* **Izaak Walton** £2.50

A celebration of the countryside, and the superiority of those in 1653, as now, who love *quietnesse, vertue* and, above all, *Angling*. 'No fish, however coarse, could wish for a doughtier champion than Izaak Walton' – Lord Home

☐ *The Portrait of a Lady* **Henry James** £2.50

'One of the two most brilliant novels in the language', according to F. R. Leavis, James's masterpiece tells the story of a young American heiress, prey to fortune-hunters but not without a will of her own.

☐ *Hangover Square* **Patrick Hamilton** £3.50

Part love story, part thriller, and set in the publands of London's Earls Court, this novel caught the conversational tone of a whole generation in the uneasy months before the Second World War.

☐ *The Rainbow* **D. H. Lawrence** £2.50

Written between *Sons and Lovers* and *Women in Love*, *The Rainbow* covers three generations of Brangwens, a yeoman family living on the borders of Nottinghamshire.

☐ *Vindication of the Rights of Woman*
Mary Wollstonecraft £2.95

Although Walpole once called her 'a hyena in petticoats', Mary Wollstonecraft's vision was such that modern feminists continue to go back and debate the arguments so powerfully set down here.

ENGLISH AND AMERICAN LITERATURE IN PENGUINS

☐ **Nostromo** **Joseph Conrad** £1.95

In his most ambitious and successful novel Conrad created an entire imaginary republic in South America. As he said, 'you shall find there according to your deserts: encouragement, consolation, fear, charm – all you demand – and, perhaps, also that glimpse of truth for which you forgot to ask.'

☐ **A Passage to India** **E. M. Forster** £2.50

Centred on the unsolved mystery at the Marabar Caves, Forster's masterpiece conveys, as no other novel has done, the troubled spirit of India during the Raj.

These books should be available at all good bookshops or newsagents, but if you live in the UK or the Republic of Ireland and have difficulty in getting to a bookshop, they can be ordered by post. Please indicate the titles required and fill in the form below.

NAME _____ BLOCK CAPITALS

ADDRESS _____

_____

_____

Enclose a cheque or postal order payable to The Penguin Bookshop to cover the total price of books ordered, plus 50p for postage. Readers in the Republic of Ireland should send £1R equivalent to the sterling prices, plus 67p for postage. Send to: The Penguin Bookshop, 54/56 Bridlesmith Gate, Nottingham, NG1 2GP.

You can also order by phoning (0602) 599295, and quoting your Barclaycard or Access number.

Every effort is made to ensure the accuracy of the price and availability of books at the time of going to press, but it is sometimes necessary to increase prices and in these circumstances retail prices may be shown on the covers of books which may differ from the prices shown in this list or elsewhere. This list is not an offer to supply any book.

This order service is only available to residents in the UK and the Republic of Ireland.

● ● ●